RETHINKING DRUG COURTS

The International Drug Policy Unit (IDPU) is a cross-regional and multi-disciplinary research unit, designed to establish a global centre for excellence in the study of international drug policy. It is based at the LSE's United States Centre, at the London School of Economics and Political Science (LSE). By utilising LSE's academic expertise and networks, the IDPU fosters new research, analysis and debate around global drug policies. Working closely with governments and policymakers around the world, we help design, implement and evaluate new policies at local, national, regional and international levels.

The IDPU hosts the *Journal of Illicit Economies and Development* (LSE Press), a peer-reviewed, open access, electronic journal publishing research and policy commentary on the complex relationship between illicit markets and development. The journal is cross-disciplinary and engages with academics, practitioners and decision makers in facilitating interventions and development planning that incorporates an in-depth understanding of the dynamics of illicit markets.

The IDPU Book Series seeks to foster new research and debates on key issues within international drug policy. It aims to provide the evidence base and the analyses needed for practitioners, decision makers and students in the fields of drug policy, public health, criminology, sociology, international relations and beyond.

Books in this series

Rethinking Drug Courts: International Experiences of a US Policy Export
Edited by John Collins, Winifred Agnew-Pauley and Alexander Soderholm

Rethinking Drug Courts

INTERNATIONAL EXPERIENCES
OF A US POLICY EXPORT

Edited by
John Collins, Winifred Agnew-Pauley
and Alexander Soderholm

LONDON SCHOOL OF ECONOMICS AND POLITICAL SCIENCE
LSE INTERNATIONAL DRUG POLICY UNIT

Published by London Publishing Partnership
www.londonpublishingpartnership.co.uk

Published in association with the International Drug Policy Unit
at the London School of Economics and Political Science
www.lse.ac.uk/drugpolicy

This book is the result of a project funded by the
Open Society Foundations

ISBN: 978-1-907994-85-2 (hardback)
ISBN: 978-1-907994-86-9 (ePDF)
ISBN: 978-1-907994-87-6 (ePUB)

A catalogue record for this book is available from the British Library

Typeset in Adobe Garamond Pro by T&T Productions Ltd, London
www.tandtproductions.com

Cover design by Adrianna Collins

Printed and bound by TJ International Ltd, Padstow, Cornwall

Contents

Introduction

By John Collins, Winifred Agnew-Pauley and
Alexander Soderholm

Drug courts, or drug treatment courts, or dedicated drug courts, remain a simultaneously popular, derided, evangelised, complex and generally contested intervention. They are almost universally traced back to the Miami Drug Court of the 1980s and are often seen as a direct United States (US) policy export (Csete and Tomasini-Joshi, 2015). Praised by some as revolutionary, benign and indeed lifesaving interventions that quite simply 'work!' (UNODC, 2005), they are criticised by others as mere 'window dressing' (Butler, 2013), with poor outcomes, a questionable and perhaps exploitive international political economy, and ultimately a misdirection of drug treatment efforts towards the criminal justice rather than public health system (Csete and Tomasini-Joshi, 2015). The result, as some judges have highlighted, is a tendency to foster judges undertaking 'amateur' social work or psychiatry (Butler, 2013). Others (several authors in this volume included) view drug courts – when underpinned by reasonable assumptions about their role, scale and limits – as a small but important piece of a broad diversion-based approach to drug-involved clients within court systems. Some take a more sceptical view. This volume offers a balanced, but broadly revisionist, account of the international evidence on drug courts, pointing to cases where the models have been viewed as a relative success, e.g. in Australia, juxtaposed with other environments where the courts have been portrayed as an international success when, in fact, they are seen domestically as well-meaning but ultimately failed experiments that should end, e.g. in Ireland.

Shane Butler suggests that models termed as drug courts share the following common features.

- They are primarily aimed at resolving underlying drug problems deemed to be causally responsible for criminal recidivism.
- They provide participants with a multidisciplinary treatment programme, delivered by a drug court team that is under the control of the judge.
- Participants are subject to frequent drug testing and court appearances, and are rewarded for progress and punished for relapse.
- Lawyers play little or no part in this non-adversarial court system (Butler, 2013, p. 6)

This volume seeks to wade into the continued debates over drug courts, albeit, we think, from a relatively underserved international comparative perspective. Our aim is twofold. Firstly, to re-examine the evidence base surrounding these contested interventions. Secondly, to provide a basis for evaluation for countries considering importing these interventions. Governments, particularly throughout Latin America, continue with strong support from the US government and key regional institutions to consider, adopt and expand these models, believing them to have an international evidence base that is clear and certain. This volume should at least provide pause for thought, and perhaps a case for rigorous re-evaluation of whether this model suits local needs, whether it is cost-effective, and whether, simply put, its aims could be achieved through other mechanisms. These other mechanisms could be expanded pre-booking diversion programmes, investing in low-threshold community-based social and treatment services, and ultimately moving towards a more decriminalised approach to drugs and drug-involved individuals.

From the outset this volume has been guided by an awareness of the following concerns.

1. That the evidence surrounding drug court models is systematically misrepresented at a global level so as to portray them as an unqualified success.
2. That economic interests and lobbying, rather than any overarching evidence base, have driven, and continue to drive, the international expansion of drug courts.

3. That drug courts represent an expensive system of contested efficacy. This is magnified in jurisdictions where the opportunity costs of such complex interventions are high, their likelihood of success is low, and their potential for abuses is significant.
4. That drug courts risk maintaining a criminal justice orientation to social interventions on drugs, while adopting the language and appearance of being public health oriented.
5. That interventions in many international contexts that are labelled as 'drug courts', upon closer inspection maintain only a superficial resemblance to the model as proffered by US advocates, and thereby serve to obfuscate more systematic changes underway in the field of drug control.
6. That there are significant opportunity and sunk costs for adopting jurisdictions, particularly in poorer countries, with more problematic criminal justice and social service outcomes and coverage.

METHODOLOGICAL OVERVIEWS

This volume follows a case study based approach, examining the specific experiences and outcomes of the US, Ireland, England, Scotland, Wales, Australia and Brazil, and focuses on the implementation of 'diversion' more broadly. It has been produced as a series of case studies for a number of reasons, perhaps most importantly to highlight that the experience of drug courts is not uniform. Instead, each jurisdiction has a set of experiences unique to its own context. This in itself runs counter to much of the international policy debates, which simply highlight the existence of various jurisdictions with drug court models as de facto proof of the model's success. In each case we found a mixed picture ranging from equivocal evidence, to poor outcomes, to internal collapse, to marginal efficacy in specific and limited cases. Each author's case study has been undertaken with a different methodology and approach, with varying takeaways based on national experiences. While the US case study represents a critical evaluation of a seemingly oversold evidence base, the Australian case study provides a sober and encouraging account of the evolution of a diversion and treatment programme embedded within a broad, holistic and complex series of potential interventions supported within the criminal justice system.

Meanwhile, the Brazilian case study is intended as a counterexample to a seemingly inexorable regional Latin American trend towards the adoption of the model. It highlights Brazil as a place where the model was tried but ultimately allowed to lapse. The author in that case utilises a contextual social–political–economic evaluation to provide some of the reasons why drug courts became seen as the wrong intervention for the wrong context. For the Irish and United Kingdom (UK) case studies, the author adopts an institutional analysis to explain the systemic reasons for the ultimate failure and, in some cases, collapse of the models, and thereby provides a further contextual basis for analysis for countries examining importing or expanding the model to new jurisdictions. Finally, in a more generalist criminal justice research approach, the concluding chapter critically evaluates the deeper intellectual and criminological roots of drug court interventions, charting, perhaps, a less polarised and more context- and needs-specific approach to designing interventions grounded in a diversion philosophy. Taken together, then, these contributions provide an extensive, although far from exhaustive, evaluation of the state of the drug court model in the international policy sphere.

This volume thereby highlights a variety of disciplinary approaches to thinking about and evaluating drug courts, whether based on a broad evidentiary basis, such as the US and Australian cases, or on contexts with a relatively weak evidence base but a reasonably strong qualitative literature evaluating the sociopolitical and institutional causes of failure, such as is the case for the Ireland and UK case studies. Or, as in the Brazilian case, an approach that grounds the drug courts experience within a broader overview of their socioeconomic determinants, elaborating key contextual issues relevant to any policy outcome in this field in Brazil and, most likely, in other contexts facing similar issues.

CHAPTER OVERVIEWS

In Chapter 1, Joanne Csete provides a critical evaluation of the US experiences of drug courts. She highlights that, while drug courts thrive within the US and enjoy widespread political support, decades of research has, at best, highlighted marginal efficacy in certain targeted areas. Specifically, small but not insignificant reductions in recidivism for certain groups, while demonstrating no measurable impact on levels of incarceration, despite repeated promises to achieve this. They have been the subject of a litany of complaints about cherry-picking of clients and perverse outcomes for people funnelled into the intervention, such as 'failing' and receiving a worse sentence than if they had not undertaken the programme. Further, public health experts recoil at the tendency for judges to end up making medical decisions on behalf of clients with, at times, lethal consequences, such as demanding that clients cease medication-assisted treatment (MAT) in order to qualify. Meanwhile, Csete points out that drug courts ultimately exclude such a broad section of drug-involved individuals from eligibility and are so exceptionally costly to run that they represent at best a weak policy intervention, and at worst one that is, or will be, a burden to importing jurisdictions.

In Chapter 2, Caitlin Hughes and Marian Shanahan outline the history and role of drug courts in the Australian context: as a broader criminal justice response within a continuum of diversionary responses to drugs and drug-related offending. Drug courts were first introduced in Australia in 1999 and they now operate in most of Australia's states and territories. The authors highlight that Australian drug courts have been monitored and evaluated from the time of implementation, and have shown promising outcomes in relation to reducing offending and drug use, while also improving general health and well-being in a cost-effective manner. They highlight that system mapping and clear programme logic is vital to the success of these interventions in Australia. Hughes and Shanahan demonstrate that while drug courts in Australia play a key role, they are but one of a broad range of diversionary responses to drugs and drug-related offending and thus often serve as a 'last resort' within the continuum of criminal justice responses.

In Chapter 3, John Collins provides an institutional analysis for the failure of one of Europe's first fully fledged drug court models: the Dublin Drug Treatment Court (DDTC). His chapter is intended as a broad critical literature review, drawing in particular on the work of a number of key scholars who have undertaken qualitative assessments of the DDTC. He juxtaposes these with a re-examination of government evaluations of the efficacy of the DDTC, virtually all of which have portrayed a policy intervention that is simultaneously popular and problematic in terms of its stated goals, particularly in attracting and retaining clients. Collins also provides a critical review of the constitutional position of the DDTC and suggests that the current operation poses serious due-process concerns. He concludes by highlighting that, as in so many other cases with the drug court model internationally, the programme achieves a normative support base that seeks to judge the intervention in terms of professed intentions rather than actual outcomes.

In Chapter 4, Luiz Guilherme Mendes de Paiva discusses the complex relationship between drug policy and criminal justice in Brazil. With one of the world's largest prison populations and with drug offences as the most frequent cause of arrest, Brazil's attempt to address the rising overincarceration of drug-involved individuals is a matter of urgency. Guilherme outlines the legal framework and judicial activity on this matter, including a drug court model known as the therapeutic jurisprudence programme. Underlying Brazil's 'drugs problem' is the deeply rooted inequality within the criminal justice system and in the application of the law, heightening the marginalisation of those most vulnerable in Brazilian society. As Guilherme outlines, the therapeutic jurisprudence programme, drawing largely on the US drug court model, has failed to take root in Brazil. This is a similar experience to other countries in South America and Central America, where the US drug court model has been widely promoted as the key solution to addressing drug-related crime. Poor implementation, combined with not taking into account the local circumstances of South/Central American contexts, has resulted in the development of unsuitable and unsustainable programmes. Guilherme points instead to the local-level programmes effectively operating as diversion programmes. These encourage the introduction of social support services, such as housing or drug treatment, while individuals are in contact with the criminal justice system, typically at the custody hearing stage while awaiting trial. However, despite promising results, these programmes rely on judges acknowledging that individuals coming before the court for low-level drug-related offences require social support as opposed to criminal punishment.

In Chapter 5, John Collins examines the outcomes and lessons of efforts to implement and expand dedicated drug courts (DDCs) in the UK. He looks to the differing experiences of Scotland, England and Wales, all of which appear to converge on the ultimate outcome of institutional decline or collapse. Further, this chapter seeks to question the characterisation of DDCs as a softer alternative to traditional criminal justice system approaches. Collins highlights that the evidence from England paints an ambivalent picture, with some DDCs imposing more severe penalties on clients. Meanwhile, the quantitative evidence is either insufficient to draw conclusions or simply suggests a picture of failed institutional scale-up. As with Ireland, he suggests, the UK drug courts run into the fallacy of optimal expectations, basing the belief in their efficacy on how they 'should' work, and 'would' if functioning correctly, according to an abstract set of international principles. The UK, he continues, provides yet another example of an intervention that is imported from an extreme context: the US 'War on Drugs'. It is then imposed in an institutional, bureaucratic, cultural and social situation that ultimately rejects the model, despite repeated and strong political support from the highest levels of government and many criminal justice organisations. Although perhaps well intentioned, he concludes, the UK case tells a story of importing trains to a country with the wrong type of tracks. They can be made to run briefly on a temporary construction, but ultimately they will fail to merge with the existing national infrastructure.

In Chapter 6, Winifred Agnew-Pauley critically examines the use of diversion programmes within the criminal justice system (CJS) and gives an overview of key lessons learned from existing international research. Diversion covers a broad range of police and court-based interventions designed to provide an alternative outcome to traditional criminal justice responses. It aims to balance a dual function to first '*divert away* from the CJS via an alternative procedure to traditional criminal justice processing, and second, to *divert into* programmes or services aimed at addressing drug use and offending behaviour', drawing on theories of true diversion, therapeutic jurisprudence and harm reduction. The drug courts model, as a court-led intervention, has largely dominated as the key method of diversion. However, in order to be most effective, states ought to operate with a range of diversionary programmes that target low-risk individuals at the police level, and higher-risk, higher-needs individuals at the court level. Programmes ought to follow best-practice standards in terms of programme design, delivery, operation and monitoring, and be mindful of net-widening. Furthermore, Agnew-Pauley argues for the need for more robust and methodologically strong evidence and evaluations of diversion programmes. Implementation of diversion programmes demands an understanding of the complex relationship between drugs and crime, and in turn a social approach towards addressing drug use, as opposed to an approach based strictly on criminal justice. Further, she argues for an appreciation of the local contexts in which diversion programmes operate, setting clear and appropriate targets and realistic outcomes.

CONCLUSIONS

While drug court 'successes' are often portrayed as a product of much needed 'tough love' towards clients, the key insight and theme that emerges consistently from research on demand-side interventions is the centrality of coherent and low-threshold wraparound services. In the case of US drug courts, as Timothy Casey describes, these alternative courts found a toehold where existing social or legal institutions had proven woefully inadequate or had failed altogether (Casey, 2004). When applied in Ireland, the

UK and in other contexts, drug courts were transplanted into an unsuitable legal system within a complex institutional ecosystem of deep social support structures, which were expected to adapt around the foreign plant. This simply did not occur in many cases. Meanwhile, those international drug court models that did take root and have demonstrated the most efficacy have shown a number of key underpinnings.

1. An exceptionally integrated interaction between public health, social and welfare services that address the underlying marginalisation and health issues of the individuals involved. In the Americas this is rarely the operating norm and should be recognised as such when contemplating the drug court model.
2. That these courts represent an absolute last recourse for complex cases already involved in the criminal justice system. Thus, they may appear as drug courts in name, but are ultimately part of a complex set of interventions intended to extricate the individual who has, through a failure of social support services, ended up in the criminal justice system. The latter, it is recognised, frequently only serves to exacerbate their vulnerabilities. However, under the current construction, drug court models too often tend to net-widen and bring individuals into the criminal justice system rather than divert them away from it.
3. The courts operate in a reasonably decentralised criminal justice system, which enables the court to develop close operating relationships with necessary social services that can assume key responsibilities. In contexts such as parts of Australia, this has been shown to be relatively effective. In many other contexts, it has not. In the US, this frequently manifests as judges simply dictating treatment regimens without adequate consultation of health professionals or knowledge of the science of drug dependence. Further, judges punish clients for 'failing'. In other contexts, this has simply resulted in policy failure. In the UK, the need for decentralised courts and services proved too high a threshold in a highly centralised system, and the number of drug courts collapsed precipitously. In Ireland, clients found the courts

to be short-term fixes that provided little in the way of prolonged wrap-around services, which they may have received had they not been funnelled into a rigid criminal justice system.

For these reasons we suggest deep caution and reticence on the part of Latin American governments to welcome the import of these models. The case study we have examined in Latin America suggests a predictable outcome based on the above cautionary tales. Meanwhile, the legal infrastructure being created will eventually pose a direct cost to the state, at an opportunity cost of more effective, evidence-based, low-threshold community treatment interventions. Further, the propensity for human rights abuses is present to such a degree that, in light of the academic evidence available, we suggest against their continued roll-out to areas without the fundamental oversight and monitoring components necessary.

This edited volume in no way suggests that drug courts are a universally flawed intervention. Instead, it seeks to shed new and much-needed critical light on the existing evidence and experience with the models, as well as on their potential for abuse and unintended outcomes when being imported into complex contexts. Ultimately, jurisdictions must evaluate whether the model contains elements that are replicable and desirable given their local exigencies and capacities. What this book highlights is that the fundamental principles of diversion and decriminalisation of drug use are a key trajectory for drug policy implementation and reform globally. Whether drug courts assist or distract from this goal remains a topic for debate. Ultimately, based on the balance of evidence and experience contained within these national case studies, we as the editors of this volume suggest a move away from the drug court model as a mechanism for framing diversion discussions. Instead, we suggest a more comprehensive move into discussions of decriminalisation and diversion at all stages of the criminal justice system. Alongside this, and in line with the recommendations contained within the UN General Assembly Special Session on Drugs 2016 outcome document, we suggest a reinvigorated and constant drive towards expanding, consolidating and innovating on public-health-driven and harm-reduction-oriented responses to drug use and drug dependence. Within these recommendations remains the old adage that there are no silver bullets, and policymakers should retain healthy scepticism when considering models that appear to offer them.

REFERENCES

Butler, S. (2013). The symbolic politics of the Dublin drug court: the complexities of policy transfer. *Drugs Educ. Prev. Policy* 20, 5–13.

Casey, T. (2004). *When Good Intentions Are Not Enough: Problem-Solving Courts and the Impending Crisis of Legitimacy.* Southern Methodist University Law Review, Volume 57.

Csete, J., and Tomasini-Joshi, D. (2015). *Drug Courts: Equivocal Evidence on a Popular Intervention.* Open Society Foundations, New York.

UNODC (2005). *Drug Treatment Courts Work!* United Nations Office on Drugs and Crime, Vienna.

About the editors and authors

THE EDITORS

Dr John Collins is Executive Director of the International Drug Policy Unit (IDPU) at the London School of Economics and Political Science (LSE), a Fellow of the LSE US Centre and a Distinguished Visiting Fellow of the Yale Centre for the Study of Globalization. He is Editor-in-Chief of the *Journal of Illicit Economies and Development* (LSE Press). He is currently a Co-Investigator on a Global Challenges Research Fund project examining illicit drug economies in the borderlands of Myanmar, Afghanistan and Colombia, and Project Investigator on a major Open Society Foundations Institutional Support grant focusing on drugs and sustainable development. He earned a PhD from the Department of International History at the London School of Economics looking at Anglo-American relations and international drug control over the period 1939–1964.

Winifred Agnew-Pauley has a background in criminology and has worked as a researcher across a range of criminal justice projects in Australia and in the UK. She currently works as a Researcher at Anglia Ruskin University within the Policing Institute for the Eastern Region (PIER). Previously, she has worked for the New South Wales Bureau of Crime Statistics and Research in Sydney, the Department of Security and Crime Science at University College London, and the International Drug Policy Unit (IDPU) at the LSE. Her research interests focus on how drugs are dealt with in the criminal justice system and street-level policing, specifically illicit drug policy, drug law enforcement, stop and search practices and social bias in the criminal justice system.

Alexander Soderholm is the Policy Coordinator of the International Drug Policy Unit at the London School of Economics and Political Science (LSE), and the Managing Editor of the *Journal of Illicit Economies and Development* (LSE Press). He holds an MSc in International Development and Humanitarian Emergencies and is currently a PhD Candidate in the LSE Department of Social Policy, studying drug policy and drug markets in the Islamic Republic of Iran. He has worked in a number of international contexts on issues related to drugs and development, including the United Nations Office on Drugs and Crime in Tehran. His research focuses on the intersection between drug markets and development outcomes, specifically on questions related to harm reduction and health, livelihoods and security.

THE AUTHORS

Dr Joanne Csete is on the faculty of the Mailman School of Public Health of Columbia University, New York. She was previously deputy director of the Global Drug Policy Programme of the Open Society Foundations, executive director of the Canadian HIV/AIDS Legal Network, and founding director of the HIV Programme at Human Rights Watch. She worked on health programmes in Africa for over 10 years, including in the UNICEF Regional Office for Eastern and Southern Africa, and has written extensively on access to health services for criminalised persons.

Dr Luiz Guilherme Mendes de Paiva holds an MSc and a PhD in criminal law from the University of São Paulo. As a federal civil servant in Brazil, he was the Head of the Secretariat for Drug Policy at the Ministry of Justice (2015/2016). Among other relevant positions, he was Special Advisor to the President of the Federal Supreme Court of Brazil and a member of the National Council for Criminal and Penitentiary Policy, responsible for overseeing prison conditions in the country. He is currently the Coordinator for Legislative Affairs at the Brazilian Institute for Criminal

Sciences, and a regular participant at national and international forums on drug policy.

Dr Caitlin Hughes is a criminologist and Senior Research Fellow at the National Drug and Alcohol Research Centre, University of New South Wales in Australia, where she works as part of the Drug Policy Modelling Program. Her research focuses on drug laws and criminal justice policies: identifying 'what works' and avenues for more effective policy responses. She works with policymakers and police to aid research translation. Dr Hughes has over 70 peer reviewed articles, book chapters and reports. Her research has also contributed to policy change within and outside Australia, including the expansion of drug diversion programmes and reform of drug trafficking laws.

Dr Marian Shanahan is a Senior Research Fellow at the National Drug and Alcohol Research Centre, University of New South Wales in Australia. As a health economist she has applied health economics principles to evaluating a diverse range of treatments, interventions and structural issues in the alcohol and illicit drugs field. Her research activities have utilised economic evaluation tools (cost effectiveness, cost utility and cost–benefit analyses) to address policy questions and inform policymakers. She has published widely in both the peer reviewed literature and reports for government bodies and other agencies.

RETHINKING DRUG COURTS

CHAPTER 1

Drug Courts in the United States: Punishment for 'Patients'?

By Joanne Csete

A central theme of the 2016 United Nations General Assembly Special Session (UNGASS) on the 'world drug problem' was the need for governments to see minor, non-violent drug infractions – particularly simple use and possession of minor amounts – as health concerns rather than matters to be dealt with by the use of criminal sanctions (United Nations General Assembly [UNGA], 2016a). That is, as many of the government representatives at the Special Session put it: people who use drugs and others where addiction is part of the reason for comitting a crime should be regarded as 'patients, not criminals' (UNGA, 2016b). The unanimous outcome statement from the UNGASS encouraged countries, within the constraints of their legal systems and their treaty obligations, to implement 'alternatives or additional measures with regards to conviction or punishment in cases of an appropriate nature' (UNGA, 2016a, Paragraph 4.j).

In 2016 the United States (US) was among the United Nations (UN) member states espousing a more health-oriented and less prison-oriented approach to drug dependence and related problems. In the view of US government officials, at least through early 2017, the US's move to more health-oriented management of drug use and related infractions was well represented by specialised drug treatment courts (hereinafter 'drug courts') (US Office of National Drug Control Policy [US ONDCP], 2014; Pelley, 2015). Drug courts are meant to offer court-supervised treatment for drug dependence in cases where drug dependence is deemed to be an underlying determinant of a non-violent criminal act. In the US, the accused persons in question would likely otherwise be incarcerated; drug courts are meant to divert them from this fate. Thus, drug courts, in theory, offer both an alternative to incarceration for certain drug infractions and a means to address drug dependence as a cause of drug-related crime.

As discussed in this chapter, drug courts are widespread and politically very popular in the US. The US government has made the promotion of and support for drug courts in other countries a centrepiece of its drug-related foreign policy. The purpose of this chapter is to examine the reality of the US drug court experience with an eye to identifying whether these special courts constitute a just and effective alternative to incarceration and whether they realise their objective to provide appropriate medical services to those in their charge.

US DRUG COURTS: HISTORY AND EVOLUTION OF THE MODEL

Addressing mass incarceration

That the US leads the world in per-capita incarceration is a well-documented phenomenon of long standing. The 'War on Drugs' is far from the only factor contributing to mass incarceration in the US, but it is an important one. From 1980 to 1989 alone, the number of people convicted for drug-related crimes in state (as opposed to federal) prisons increased more than fivefold (Franco, 2010). In 1980, drug-related offenders represented 6% of people in state prison systems; in 2006, the figure was 20% (Franco, 2010, p. 4). The number of people incarcerated for drug-related offences overall in both state and federal systems was about 41,000 in 1980 and about 470,000 in 2015, an increase driven in part by mandatory minimum sentences for a wide range of drug infractions, including non-violent offences (Sentencing Project, 2017).

The first drug court, established in 1989 in the state of Florida, was meant to respond to this dramatic rise in the number of drug-related offenders entering the justice system. It also aimed to address judges' perceptions that many people were cycling through the courts with repeated offences that were linked to unresolved drug dependence (National Association of Drug Court Professionals [NADCP], n.d.). It was thought that through combining 'the coercive power of the criminal justice system' with treatment for drug dependence, problematic substance use, and thus also the crimes associated with it, might be reduced (Franco, 2010). From that time, drug courts spread rapidly across the country. By 2001 there were over 1,000 drug courts (Douglas and Hartley, 2004), and by mid-2016, there were an estimated 3,057 drug courts in the US (NADCP, 2016). The non-partisan Congressional Research Service (CRS), a research agency linked to the US Library of Congress that works exclusively for the US Congress, characterised this growth as a 'movement' since, especially in the early years, it was not based on empirical evidence of the benefit of the courts (Franco, 2010).

Drug courts have also become a pillar of drug-related US foreign policy. The US has been a key supporter of an effort by the Organization of American States (OAS) to set up drug courts and related 'problem-solving courts' in Central and South America and Mexico (US Department of State, 2016). In 2013, the OAS reported that there were drug courts in Argentina, Barbados, Bermuda, Chile, Colombia, Costa Rica, the Dominican Republic, Mexico, Panama, Peru and Trinidad and Tobago, as well as the US and Canada (OAS, 2013). There are also drug treatment courts of some kind in Australia, New Zealand, Belgium, Norway, Austria, the UK and Ireland (Marlowe *et al.*, 2016, p. 61).

The National Association of Drug Court Professionals (NADCP), a non-governmental organisation that promotes drug courts and issues standards for their operation, describes drug courts as 'a sentencing alternative providing life-saving treatment to people living with substance use and mental health disorders, offering a public health response to addiction within the criminal justice system' (NADCP, 2016, n.p.). It might be supposed from this description that every effort is made in these courts to keep participants (the accused) focused on treatment by putting them at a remove from criminal sanctions to the greatest degree possible. However, this is not the case for most US drug courts. The vast majority of drug courts in the US offer court-supervised treatment only after a person has made a plea to a criminal charge and appeared before a judge – that is, post-adjudication (Franco, 2010; Marlowe *et al.*, 2016). In the early years of drug courts, there were more pre-adjudication programmes – that is, ones that offered entry into a treatment programme before a charge is 'booked' or entered into the record. In the dominant post-adjudication model, most drug courts require participants to plead guilty. That practice means that if for some reason a person is unable to complete the drug-court-supervised treatment programme successfully, he or she may be redirected to normal criminal courts, where the prior guilty plea means no opportunity to engage in plea-bargaining. Post-adjudication models are also less likely to offer expungement of the criminal record to drug court 'graduates', even to people with no prior convictions (National Association of Criminal Defense Lawyers [NACDL], 2009).

There are virtually no binding rules to govern drug court operations, including the kind of treatment they offer, the way in which drug court staff engage (or not) with health professionals, or the frequency of participants' required court appearances or mandatory drug tests. All of these factors are determined largely by the presiding judge. As noted by one drug courts scholar, these courts are defined by 'a model where the judge is the central figure in the recovery process' (Tiger, 2011, p. 177). As a result, drug court processes vary somewhat from jurisdiction to jurisdiction. A common feature of most drug courts, however, is that the usual adversarial roles of the prosecutor and defence attorney are abandoned as all of these parties become part of a team meant to support the participant through the court-supervised treatment programme. Mandatory, random and repeated drug testing (urinalysis) is also generally used to monitor treatment adherence, and relatively frequent appearances before the court are standard. These are among the 'key components' of drug courts recommended by the NADCP and the US government (US Department of Justice [DoJ], 1997).

In the US, the drug courts helped to usher in a wider phenomenon of establishing 'problem-solving' courts of various kinds, including courts for persons convicted of driving while intoxicated, mental health courts, domestic violence courts and special courts for veterans of the armed forces. According to the federal government's monitoring of these courts, about two-thirds of them require a guilty plea to be entered before the accused person can participate in diversionary treatment in any of these areas (Strong et al., 2016).

Evaluations of the US drug courts: methodological challenges

A large and widely cited evaluation of US drug courts is the 2011 multi-site adult drug court evaluation (Rossman et al., 2011), financed by the US National Institute of Justice (NIJ), a government agency that also gives grants to drug courts. Covering 23 courts in six sites, this study found lower self-reported rates of having committed a crime among drug court 'graduates' in the 24 months after being in court and lower official re-arrest rates, though the difference in the latter was not statistically significant. The drug court participants were significantly less likely to report using all drugs in the two years after court supervision, and this was also the case for 'hard' drugs – that is, drugs other than marijuana and alcohol. The drug court group had significantly lower prevalence of positive drug tests (buccal swab) 18 months after leaving the court (29% versus 46%) (Rossman et al., 2011).

Drug court evaluations, however, face considerable methodological challenges. In 2011 the non-partisan US Government Accountability Office (GAO), a federal auditing agency, reviewed 260 drug court evaluations, most of them studying recidivism as the outcome of interest. This included the NIJ's six-site evaluation. Of the 260 studies it reviewed, the GAO concluded that only 44 studies (20%) used sound social science methods (GAO, 2011). A 'lack of equivalent comparison groups' was one of the main concerns raised by the GAO (GAO, 2011, p. 9), valid comparison groups being an important pillar of any attempt to make causal conclusions about drug court impact. This concern is hardly surprising since so many elements of the drug court experience differ significantly from what people in other parts of the justice system experience. An evaluation design with random allocation of persons to drug courts (or another fate) would also be ideal for making causal conclusions. However, randomisation of people is generally not possible, and if it is possible it would raise ethical concerns. The GAO nonetheless concluded that 56% of the methodologically valid studies suggested that drug court participation was associated with a reduction in re-arrest rates (GAO, 2011, p. 19). Meanwhile, in the CRS's review of drug court evaluations in 2010, the methodological difficulties of evaluating these institutions was also highlighted. The CRS also noted that many evaluations do not try to take into account the people who drop out of drug court programmes without completing treatment, who are numerous in most jurisdictions.

Other concerns about the drug court model

Other evaluations and analyses of drug court experiences have suggested a range of problems associated with the US model of these specialised courts and their claims of positive transformation of the lives of people who use drugs.

Lack of provision of appropriate treatment

At the time of writing, the US is in the midst of a historic crisis of opioid overdose mortality. The estimated 63,000 opioid overdose deaths in 2016 was more than triple the rate in 1999 on a per-capita basis. The age-adjusted rate of overdoses increased by an average of 10% annually from 1999 to 2006, 3% from 2006 to 2014, and 18% annually from 2014 to 2016 (Hedegaard *et al.*, 2017). In such a situation, it should be a priority for all institutions in contact with people living with opioid dependence to make the greatest possible range of scientifically sound treatments available, with as few obstacles to access as possible. The drug courts, however, have a long history of denying access to opioid dependence treatment that is scientifically proven and effective, in many cases supposedly because of the belief of judges or drug court coordinators that methadone or buprenorphine maintenance therapy is no better than dependence on illicit drugs (Matusow *et al.*, 2013; Physicians for Human Rights, 2017). In some cases, people already receiving medication-assisted treatment (MAT) with methadone or buprenorphine are required to 'taper off' and stop this therapy in an arbitrary period of time as a condition of drug court participation (Csete and Catania, 2013; Physicians for Human Rights, 2017).

Federal authorities recognised this problem and in 2015 issued a notice that federal funding would not be available to drug courts that 'deny any eligible client for the drug court access to the program because of their use of FDA [Food and Drug Administration]-approved medications for the treatment of substance use disorders' (DoJ, 2015, p. 6). The statement continued:

> Specifically, methadone treatment rendered in accordance with current federal and state methadone dispensing regulations from an Opioid Treatment Program and ordered by a physician who has evaluated the client and determined that methadone is an appropriate medication treatment for the individual's opioid use disorder must be permitted.   (US Department of Justice, 2015, pp. 6–7)

It is difficult to assess the impact of this policy, but the political popularity of drug courts in some jurisdictions may allow for state, county or municipal funding for courts that are functioning in the absence of federal funds in case judges wish to continue to deny MAT for opioid dependence. The impact of that denial can be disastrous. Treatment providers in New York noted that people required to stop methadone maintenance therapy are likely to seek illicit and dangerous opioids on the street, and in some cases they expressed despair that judges were making medical decisions for which they were unqualified (Csete and Catania, 2013). In its investigation of drug court practices in three states, the non-governmental organisation Physicians for Human Rights found that:

Diagnosis and initial treatment plans for drug court participants were often developed by people with no medical training or oversight, at times resulting in mandated treatment that was at odds with medical knowledge and recommendations.

(Physicians for Human Rights, 2017, p. 3)

Investigative reporting in Kentucky recounted numerous cases of dangerous relapses and worse among people denied MAT by drug courts (Cherkis, 2015). Cherkis cited the view of one Kentucky judge who does not allow MAT as a treatment option in her court: 'I understand they are talking about harm reduction; those things don't work in the criminal justice system. It sounds terrible, but I don't give them a choice. This is the structure that I'm comfortable with' (2015, n.p). It is true that in many US counties there are simply not enough providers of MAT to meet the demand, with or without drug courts (Physicians for Human Rights, 2017). However, in these environments it is unhelpful for influential justice officials to disparage therapies that can be life-saving for many at a time of great need.

Unlike in much of Europe, in many US jurisdictions cannabis offences dominate drug-related arrests and criminal charges (Sentencing Project, 2017). With the legalisation of recreational use of cannabis in more US states, this dominance will likely fade, but for now cannabis offenders find themselves in drug treatment courts in many states. New York doctors specialising in drug dependence told Physicians for Human Rights that many people brought into drug courts on cannabis possession charges showed no signs of dependence but were forced to go through treatment designed for dependence on 'hard' drugs, even as many other defendants who were 'literally dying' for treatment were unable to get it (Physicians for Human Rights, 2017). In some cases, people in drug courts for minor cannabis offences are required to pay for lengthy residential treatment that is not appropriate to their situation (Halper, 2014). Some drug court personnel have reported, however, that they are constrained in their choice of treatments by what can be covered by health insurance or Medicaid (Physicians for Human Rights, 2017).

It is a well-recognised principle of good practice in treating drug dependence that medical interventions have a greater chance of succeeding if they are accompanied by attention to basic needs such as housing, education, employment and connections to welfare benefits (World Health Organization [WHO] and UN Office on Drugs and Crime [UNODC], 2008). Tiger (2011) notes that drug court judges, in making decisions about whether a defendant is ready to 'graduate' from the drug court, regularly assess their housing and job situations, and even their social contacts and dating practices, but these are not necessarily areas where the drug courts provide support or links to sustained services. Physician for Human Rights (2017) drew a similar conclusion from its investigation.

Incarceration for treatment 'failure' undermines the central goal of the courts

In addition to failing to provide proven and clinically indicated treatment, some drug court judges seem persuaded that punishment, including incarceration, is a fitting response to relapse for people being treated for drug dependence. The WHO defines drug dependence as a chronic, relapsing condition (WHO and UNODC, 2008). Relapse is part of the process of managing drug dependence. UN standards assert that people may need to try several kinds of treatment or several episodes of treatment to overcome drug dependence (WHO and UNODC, 2008). Or, as the American Society for Addiction Medicine (ASAM) puts it: 'Like other chronic diseases, addiction often involves cycles of relapse and remission' (ASAM, 2018, n.p.). However, many drug court judges believe that an appropriate response to relapse is punishment. Such punishment can take the form of short periods of incarceration, being dismissed from the programme and redirected to a traditional adversarial court, or requiring more frequent drug tests, which often have to be paid for by the patient themselves (Physicians for Human Rights, 2017).

A peer-reviewed 2013 meta-analysis of 19 studies from around the country found that drug courts reduced the number of incidents of incarceration but did not significantly reduce the time that their participants spent in jail or prison, partly because of punishment for 'failed' treatment that took the form of incarceration (Sevigny *et al.*, 2013). As already noted, US drug courts generally require a guilty plea as a condition of drug court participation. If people who 'fail' treatment are reverted to the regular courts, their guilty plea makes it impossible for them to engage in plea-bargaining, as might normally happen in cases of non-violent drug offences. Thus, a final prison sentence for someone who 'fails' treatment may be longer than if the defendant had never been through a drug treatment court.

'Cherry-picking' participants

As with the matter of minor cannabis infractions (described above), many observers have raised questions about whether the drug courts are including adequate numbers of people and targeting the people who need them the most. The CRS criticised drug courts both for miscounting the number of people they serve and, even allowing for possible counting errors, for serving a very small number of those who might in theory benefit from them (Franco, 2010). Drug courts vary in the criteria by which they admit defendants. In addition to simple resource constraints, most drug courts exclude people with any violent offence in their past and any prior parole or probation violations. In addition, some exclude people with any mental illness in their past (or present) or any 'acute health conditions' and favour those who are 'treatment-ready' (Sevigny *et al.*, 2013). Many drug courts also exclude people who have ever been charged or convicted with drug sales or distribution, even though it is common that people who use drugs and who are not major drug traffickers engage in small-scale sales at some time to support their own drug use (Mitchell *et al.*, 2012; Physicians for Human Rights, 2017).

In a 2013 study, Sevigny and colleagues examined the criteria by which drug courts exclude and include participants and the constraints under which those decisions are made. Based on a large body of data on recently incarcerated persons, they concluded that only 11–17% of persons recently incarcerated for drug offences would have a greater than 50/50 chance of being eligible and admitted to a drug court (Sevigny *et al.*, 2013, p. 206). In addition, the authors note that mandatory minimum sentencing laws in some states (e.g. three-strikes laws) and other sentencing enhancement factors would exclude some 30% of recently incarcerated people regardless of other eligibility criteria. Thus, they note, for drug courts to make a real dent in the huge prison populations in the US, some combination of expanding eligibility requirements and changing drug law and sentencing rules at the state level would likely be needed.

Sevigny and colleagues also speculate, as others have done, about whether drug courts limit eligibility as a way to ensure that evaluations of their work will be positive (Sevigny *et al.*, 2013). Some critics have charged that people are brought into drug courts more on the basis of whether they can pay all the treatment fees than on whether they have real drug dependence problems (Tyler, 2017). A study from the state of Delaware that used data from drug tests (urinalysis), rather than only self-reporting, concluded that about a third of the observed drug court participants did not have a verifiable drug dependence problem when they were brought into the drug courts (DeMatteo *et al.*, 2009).

Unclear cost implications

Many evaluations of drug courts compare the per-defendant cost of the drug court programme with the cost of incarcerating the same person for an assumed period. In its review of drug court evaluations, the GAO found 11 studies that it judged to have made valid cost analyses, and their findings ranged from a positive benefit of over $47,000 per drug court participant to a net cost (negative benefit) of $7,000 (GAO, 2011). The three studies of the 11 that reported a negative benefit of drug courts used drug courts mostly as an alternative to probation, rather than as an alternative to prison. Some studies may have overestimated the benefits by failing to investigate whether there was a net reduction in time of incarceration, as noted above. It would be useful to have a standardised and independently monitored means of accounting for the costs and benefits of drug courts, including the cost to people of being punished for 'failing' treatment and of being denied clinically indicated treatment.

Race and the drug courts

In the US, the overwhelmingly disproportionate arrest, conviction and incarceration of African-Americans and Hispanic Americans compared with whites are well documented (Sentencing Project, 2017). In 2016, some 75% of drug courts responding to a survey of the government's National Drug Court Institute had data on the racial composition of drug court participants (Marlowe *et al.*, 2016). According to this data, African-Americans were severely underrepresented in the drug courts compared with their representation in arrests, convictions, incarceration and probation in the criminal justice system (Marlowe *et al.*, 2016, p. 47). In its wide-ranging critique of drug courts, the NACDL raised the concern that drug courts' admission criteria tend to exclude low-income and minority defendants and urged the courts to examine the racial impact of their admission policies (NACDL, 2009).

MORE EFFECTIVE ALTERNATIVES TO INCARCERATION?

The political popularity of drug courts in the US may draw policy attention away from exploring other possible means of diverting drug defendants from incarceration and into appropriate health and social services. The experience of a number of European and Latin American countries shows that, without social disruption, laws can divert people from prison by completely removing minor use and possession offences from criminal sanctions and making them administrative offences or triggers for referral to social services (Global Commission on Drug Policy, 2014). In most US jurisdictions, politicians' fear of being perceived as 'soft on crime' sours the environment for this kind of legislative change. However, in 2000, voters in California adopted by referendum the so-called Proposition 36. This measure provides for diversion from criminal sanctions to 'court-approved' (but not court-supervised) community-based treatment for all non-violent drug offenders up to a third conviction, after which they could face a maximum of 30 days in prison. As of 2008, this policy had resulted in referral of over 300,000 people to community-based treatment, a figure far in excess of that handled by the state's drug courts in the same period (Urada *et al.*, 2009).

It is difficult to compare the impact of Proposition 36 with that of drug courts, partly because Proposition 36 is available to all people convicted of non-violent drug offences while the drug courts have rigorous admission criteria, as noted above; the populations served by the two are thus very different. One effort to make some comparisons by selecting populations with similar characteristics found (somewhat) similar outcomes from the two interventions in relapse and recidivism, but because of its wider scale, Proposition 36 resulted in much greater diversion from incarceration (Evans *et al.*, 2014). Proposition 36 was also less costly per capita partly because the duration of treatment was not generally as lengthy as that of the drug courts.

In a programme known as Law Enforcement-Assisted Diversion (LEAD) tried in a number of US cities, police who encounter people who have committed low-level drug infractions can divert them to community-based health and social services rather than to the criminal justice system (Law Enforcement Assisted Diversion (LEAD) King County, 2016). Unlike drug courts, the LEAD diversion occurs before any charges are laid – 'pre-booking' in US terms – so there are no guilty pleas to face if the accused person does end up in the courts. Randomised allocation of accused persons to LEAD and non-LEAD groups was built into the pilot design in Seattle, the first city to institute LEAD, to enable rigorous evaluation of the impact of the programme. Some of the findings from evaluations of the Seattle programme so far include the following.

- LEAD participants were 60% less likely than controls to be arrested in the six months following the intervention. Over a period of about five years, the LEAD group was 58% less likely to be arrested than the controls and 39% less likely to be charged with a felony, and thus much less likely to be incarcerated (Collins *et al.*, 2015a).

- LEAD participants with precarious housing were 89% more likely than their counterparts in the control group to have secured permanent housing in the 18 months following their first encounter with the programme. They were 46% more likely to be employed or in vocational training and 33% more likely to be receiving government benefits to which they were entitled (Clifasefi *et al.*, 2016).
- The LEAD programme was estimated to cost $899 per person per month when the program started, a cost that later declined to $532 per person per month. But since the LEAD participants were so much less likely to be incarcerated or otherwise find themselves in the criminal justice system in the 18 months after the intervention, it is estimated that the program saved $2100 per participant (Collins *et al.*, 2015b).
- LEAD participants told the evaluators that they especially appreciated the 'one-stop shop' nature of the programme – providing health, housing, education, employment and other assistance – and that the programme did not require abstinence to begin helping participants. They said they felt that they participated meaningfully in decisions made about available services (Clifasefi and Collins, 2016).

More research will be needed as the LEAD programme is established in more cities, but these first evaluation results are promising. LEAD's provision of a range of health and social services is especially noteworthy.

CONCLUSIONS

There is no doubt that many people have been helped by drug courts. Each court seems to have an ample collection of stories of lives transformed with the help of the stern presence of the drug court judge and the fear of punishment for failing treatment. It is unclear, however, that these expensive institutions are well character-ised as part of a public health approach to drug control or that they justify their cost. Conferring the power to make important medical decisions to persons who are not medically trained is hardly good public health practice. Institutionalising coercion in the treatment of drug dependence, where relapse can be punished by incarceration, is decidedly bad practice, even if it 'works' for some people. Requiring guilty pleas as a condition for treatment is contrary to the idea of 'patients, not criminals' and raises due-process concerns. As Rebecca Tiger observes, drug courts 'articulate an enhanced role for the court as an institution that uses punitive power to coerce rehabilitation in the name of "helping" people' (Tiger, 2011, p. 193). Neither public health nor justice is well served in the process.

The lethal crisis of opioid overdose in the US, which has affected rural and suburban white communities as well as urban areas, has finally refuted the long-mythologised picture in the public mind of drug problems being the exclusive domain of derelict minorities in the inner cities (Hutchinson, 2017). Yet, drug policies are still based on harsh criminal penalties, and, as one observer noted, it is still easier for people living with drug dependence to get heroin than to get help (Levitz, 2017). The current situation calls for nothing short of a dramatic scaling up of health and social services for people with drug dependence, including MAT, as well as assistance with hous-ing, education and employment, and measures to ensure that they are accessible and affordable for all. Drug courts are unfortunately not a step in that direction. There is an urgent need for revisiting the drug court model in favour of more LEAD-like experiments that represent a real diversion for minor drug infractions from the ham-mer of punishment to the helping hand of supportive services.

REFERENCES

American Society for Addiction Medicine (2018). Definition of addiction. Available at https://www.asam.org/quality-practice/definition-of-addiction.

Cherkis, J. (2015). Dying to be free: there's a treatment for heroin that actually works. Why aren't we using it? *Huffington Post*, 28 January. Available at http://projects.huffingtonpost.com/dying-to-be-free-heroin-treatment.

Clifasefi, S. L., and Collins, S. E. (2016). *LEAD Program Evaluation: Describing LEAD Case Management in Participants' Own Words.* Seattle.

Clifasefi, S. L., Lonczak, H. S., and Collins, S. E. (2016). *LEAD Program Evaluation: The Impact of LEAD on Housing, Employment and Income/Benefits.* Seattle.

Collins, S. E., Lonczak, H. S., and Clifasefi, S. L. (2015a). *LEAD Program Evaluation: Recidivism Report.* Seattle.

Collins, S. E., Lonczak, H. S., and Clifasefi, S. L. (2015b). *LEAD Program Evaluation Report: Criminal Justice and Legal System Utilization and Associated Costs.* Seattle.

Csete, J., and Catania, H. (2013). Methadone treatment providers' views of drug court policy and practice: a case study of New York State. *Harm Reduction Journal* 10(1), 35 (doi: 10.1186/1477-7517-10-35).

DeMatteo, D., *et al.* (2009). Outcome trajectories in drug court: do all participants have serious drug problems? *Criminal Justice and Behavior* 36(4), 354–368 (doi: 10.1177/0093854809331547).

Douglas, J. W., and Hartley, R. E. (2004). Sustaining drug courts in Arizona and South Carolina: an experience in hodgepodge budgeting. *Justice System Journal* 25, 75–86.

Evans, E. *et al.* (2014). Comparative effectiveness of California's Proposition 36 and drug court programs before and after propensity score matching. *Crime and Delinquency* 60(6), 909–938 (doi: 10.1177/0011 128710382342).

Franco, C. (2010). *Drug Courts: Background, Effectiveness and Policy Issues for Congress.* Washington, DC. Available at http://fas.org/sgp/crs/misc/R41448.pdf.

Global Commission on Drug Policy (2014). *Taking Control: Pathways to Drug Policies that Work.* Geneva. Available at http://www.globalcommissionondrugs.org/reports/taking-control-pathways-to-drug-policies-that-work/.

Halper, E. (2014). Drug courts, meant to aid addicts, now a battlefield of pot politics. *Los Angeles Times*, 26 July.

Hedegaard, H., Warner, M., and Miniño, A. M. (2017). *Drug Overdose Deaths in the United States, 1999–2016*. NCHS Data Brief, No. 294 (Centers for Disease Control and Prevention). Available at https://www.cdc.gov/nchs/data/databriefs/db294.pdf.

Hutchinson, E. O. (2017). The opioid crisis in black and white. *Huffington Post*, 21 June. Available at https://www.huffingtonpost.com/entry/the-opioid-crisis-in-black-and-white_us_594a90d1e4b07cdb1933bed5.

Law Enforcement Assisted Diversion (LEAD) King County (2016). *Frequently Asked Questions*. Available at http://leadkingcounty.org/about/#faq.

Levitz, E. (2017). Why the opioid crisis could shatter Trump's coalition. *New York Magazine*, 26 October.

Marlowe, D. B., Harding, C. D., and Fox, C. L. (2016). *Painting the Current Picture: A National Report on Drug Courts and Other Problem-Solving Courts in the United States*. Washington, DC.

Matusow, H., *et al.* (2013). Medication assisted treatment in US drug courts: results from a nationwide survey of availability, barriers and attitudes. *Journal of Substance Abuse Treatment* 44(5), 473–480 (doi: 10.1016/j.jsat.2012.10.004).

Mitchell, O., *et al.* (2012). Assessing the effectiveness of drug courts on recidivism: a meta-analytic review of traditional and non-traditional drug courts. *Journal of Criminal Justice* 40(1), 60–71 (doi: 10.1016/j.jcrimjus.2011.11.009).

National Association of Criminal Defense Lawyers (2009). *America's Problem-Solving Courts: The Criminal Costs of Treatment and the Case for Reform*. Washington, DC.

National Association of Drug Court Professionals (2016). *New Report: Drug Courts Reach Milestone – 3000 Nationwide*. Washington, DC. Available at http://www.nadcp.org/PCP.

National Association of Drug Court Professionals (n.d.). *History: Justice Professionals Pursue a Vision*. Available at https://www.nadcp.org/learn/what-are-drug-courts/drug-court-history.

Organization of American States (2013). *Drug Treatment Courts: Involved Countries*. Available at http://www.cicad.oas.org/Main/Template.asp?-File=/fortalecimiento_institucional/dtca/invcountries_eng.asp.

Pelley, S. (2015). A new direction on drugs (interview with Michael Botticelli). *CBS News*, 13 December. Available at https://www.cbsnews.com/news/60-minutes-a-new-direction-on-drugs/.

Physicians for Human Rights (2017). Neither justice nor treatment: drug courts in the United States (June). Available at http://physiciansforhumanrights.org/assets/misc/phr_drugcourts_report_singlepages.pdf.

Rossman, S. B., *et al.* (2011). *The Multi-Site Adult Drug Court Evaluation: The Impact of Drug Courts*. Washington, DC. Available at https://www.ncjrs.gov/pdffiles1/nij/grants/237112.pdf.

Sentencing Project (2017). *Trends in U.S. Corrections (Fact Sheet)*. Washington, DC. Available at https://www.sentencingproject.org/publications/trends-in-u-s-corrections/.

Sevigny, E. L., Fuleihan, B. K., and Ferdik, F. V. (2013). Do drug courts reduce the use of incarceration? A meta-analysis. *Journal of Criminal Justice* 41(6), 416–425 (doi: 10.1016/j.jcrimjus.2013.06.005).

Sevigny, E. L., Pollack, H. A., and Reuter, P. (2013). Can drug courts help to reduce prison and jail populations? *Annals of the American Academy of Political and Social Science* (edited by M. L. Small and S. W. Allard) 647(1), 190–212 (doi: 10.1177/0002716213476258).

Strong, S. M., Rantala, R. R., and Kickelhahn, T. (2016). Census of problem-solving courts, 2012. *Bureau of Justice Statistics Bulletin*, no. NCJ 24 (September). Washington, DC.

Tiger, R. (2011). Drug courts and the logic of coerced treatment. *Sociological Forum* 26(1), 169–182 (doi: 10.1111/j.l 573-7861.2010.01229.x).

Tyler, J. L. (2017). Criminal justice reformers are hooked on drug courts, they should kick the habit. *The Hill*, 5 August. Available at http://thehill.com/blogs/pundits-blog/crime/345371-criminal-justice-reformers-are-hooked-on-drug-courts-they-should.

United Nations General Assembly (2016a). 30th Special Session (April 19–21), Official Record. UN documents A/S-30/PV.1–PV.6.

United Nations General Assembly (2016b). Our joint commitment to effectively addressing and countering the world drug problem. UN documents A/RES/S-30/1 (4 May).

Urada, D., *et al.* (2009). *Evaluation of Proposition 36: The Substance Abuse and Crime Prevention Act of 2000 – 2008 Report (Submitted to the California Department of Alcohol and Drug Programs)*. Los Angeles, CA.

US Department of Justice (1997). *Defining Drug Courts: The Key Components.* Washington, DC.

US Department of Justice (2015). *Adult Drug Court Discretionary Grant Program FY 2015 Competitive Grant Announcement.* Washington, DC. Available at https://www.bja.gov/funding/15drugcourtsol.pdf.

US Department of State (2016). *International Narcotics Control Strategy Report, Volume 1: Drug and Chemical Control.* Available at https://www.state.gov/documents/organization/253655.pdf.

US Government Accountability Office (2011). *Adult Drug Courts: Studies Show Courts Reduce Recidivism, but DOJ Could Enhance Future Performance Measure Revision Efforts.* Washington, DC. Available at http://www.gao.gov/assets/590/586793.pdf.

US Office of National Drug Control Policy (2014). *National Drug Control Strategy 2014.* Washington, DC. Available at https://obamawhitehouse.archives.gov/sites/default/files/ondcp/policy-and-research/ndcs_2014.pdf.

World Health Organization and UN Office on Drugs and Crime (2008). *Principles of Drug Dependence Treatment.* Vienna. Available at http://www.unodc.org/documents/drug-treatment/UNODC-WHO-Principles-of-Drug-Dependence-Treatment-March08.pdf.

CHAPTER 2

Drug Courts in Australia

By Caitlin Hughes and Marian Shanahan

This chapter outlines the use of drug courts in Australia. Australia is a federated country with eight states and territories and nine legal systems (covering the federal system and each state/territory), albeit most of the policing and administration of courts and legislation occurs in the states and territories. It is geographically a large country with a relatively small population (24 million). Drug courts were first opened in one state in Australia in 1999 and have subsequently been introduced into most of Australia's eight states and territories. As this chapter will demonstrate, while drug courts are an important part of the Australian criminal justice response to drugs, they are part of a broad range of drug diversionary responses that range from pre-arrest to post-court interventions (Hughes and Ritter, 2008). Australian drug courts typically focus on drug-dependent offenders who have committed drug-related offences, and they often serve as the last resort in the continuum of responses to drug use and drug-related offending. This means the role and target group of drug courts differ to many other countries.

This chapter will outline the history of drug courts in Australia and their role in the broader criminal justice response to drug use and drug-related offenders in Australia. It will then provide an overview of the similarities and differences between drug court models in Australia. It will conclude by outlining the evidence base and the lessons learned on what works, and what does not, for drug courts in Australia. Importantly, the Australian evidence base includes not only what works from a programme perspective (e.g. whether drug courts reduce recidivism) but also what works from a systems perspective (e.g. what requisite elements are needed to ensure drug court objectives can be realised). This has produced insights into when, for whom and in what circumstances drug courts work best, as well as in what contexts other drug diversionary options may produce better results.

HISTORY OF DRUG COURTS IN AUSTRALIA

The first Australian drug court, the NSW Drug Court, opened in February 1999 in New South Wales (NSW) under the Drug Court Act 1998 (NSW Government, 1998). It operated in Parramatta, a western suburb of Sydney, and targeted offenders residing in Western and South-Western Sydney. The NSW Drug Court came about through three means. First, though bureaucrats and politicians exploring means by which they could provide appropriate treatment options (Indermaur and Roberts, 2003), to address what was at the time a high rate of property crime attributed to a plentiful supply and use of heroin (Makkai, 2002; Payne, 2006). Second, because of broader community concerns about the inability of the traditional criminal justice response to 'break the cycle of drug-related crime' (Hughes, 2009; Shaw and Smith, 2001). Third, the apparent success of the drug court movement in the United States (US) (Indermaur and Roberts, 2003).

From the outset, the NSW Drug Court has targeted recidivist adult offenders with a long history of drug dependence and relapse who were facing a term of imprisonment (Freeman, 2003). The aims are:

- to reduce the drug dependency of eligible persons,
- to promote the re-integration of such drug-dependent persons into the community, and
- to reduce the need for such drug-dependent persons to resort to criminal activity to support their drug dependencies (NSW, 1998).

The scheme is post-adjudicative, requiring either a guilty plea or an intention to plead guilty. An initial sentence of imprisonment is imposed and then suspended for the duration of the drug court programme. Participants spend a minimum of 12 months on the programme. The key components include a commitment to a therapeutic jurisprudence approach, judicial supervision of offenders, mandatory drug treatment (residential or non-residential), random urine screens, social support (e.g. assistance looking for work) and a system of rewards and sanctions designed to ensure compliance with the programme (e.g. modifying the frequency of drug testing, imposing short periods of imprisonment, and programme termination). Programme conditions are tailored to each individual by a drug court team comprised of a Drug Court Judge, a clinical nurse, a legal aid solicitor and police and community corrections representatives (Freeman *et al.*, 2000). The programme is divided into three phases: stabilisation, consolidation and reintegration.

Phase 1 is the 'initiation' phase, in which participants are expected to commence drug treatment, reduce drug use, stabilise their physical health, cease criminal activity and identify needs and goals for social reintegration. In this phase, participants are required to undergo drug testing at least three times a week and to report back to the Drug Court once a week.

Phase 2 is the 'consolidation' phase, in which participants are expected to remain drug-free and crime-free, to maintain good health and to develop life and job skills. In this phase, testing for drug use is conducted twice weekly and report-back court appearances occur fortnightly.

Phase 3 is the 'reintegration' phase, in which participants are expected to stabilise their social and domestic environment, including establishing stable accommodation, to gain or be ready to gain employment, and to be financially responsible. In Phase 3, drug testing is conducted twice weekly and report-back court appearances are conducted monthly (NSW Drug Court, 2018).

Upon completion of the drug court a final sentence is imposed that takes into account the initial sentence and progress on the drug court.

An extensive evidence base has now developed on this court (Freeman, 2002; Freeman and Donnelly, 2005; Freeman *et al.*, 2000; Jones, 2011; Jones and Kemp, 2014; Lind *et al.*, 2002; Shanahan *et al.*, 2004; Taplin, 2002; Weatherburn *et al.*, 2008). Two of these studies have been randomised controlled trials. Results indicate that the NSW Drug Court has been successful at achieving its intended goals (see discussion below), albeit with some implementation issues during the early years.

In response to the evaluations, several changes were made to improve systems such as eligibility screening, monitoring of compliance and responses to breaches. For example, greater use is now made of police intelligence to decide who is eligible to enter the programme and in setting an offender's programme conditions. Additionally, the protocol for management of breaches has been modified to reduce the use of prison as a sanction (e.g. allowing accumulation of up to 14 days of prison time before that time is served, and allowing potential prison time to be reduced for 'good behaviour'), and the threshold for termination of participants has been lowered – to enable termination if the risk to the community is too high or if there is no further likelihood of progress on the programme (Weatherburn *et al.*, 2008).

Following the establishment of the NSW Drug Court, adult drug courts were introduced in four other states: South Australia (SA), Western Australia (WA) and Queensland (QLD) in 2000, and Victoria (VIC) in 2002, with further expansion occurring in some states (see Table 1). Of note, the NSW Drug Court expanded beyond its original site (Parramatta) to one regional community north of Sydney in 2011 and to a small programme in central Sydney in 2013, where it operates one day per week. This increased the capacity to a total of 309 participants commencing a drug court programme in New South Wales in 2016 and 243 active engagements by year end (NSW Drug Court, 2016). However, the number of drug courts has contracted in some states. Of note, in 2012, in spite of positive evaluations, all five Queensland Drug Courts were defunded and closed on the grounds of efficiency and savings measures (Freiberg *et al.*, 2016a), with a single Queensland adult drug court only reintroduced in January 2018 (Queensland Courts, 2018). This means that as of April 2018 there are a total of eight adult drug courts in Australia, operating across five states. The Australian Capital Territory (ACT) government has committed to introducing their first adult drug and alcohol court, but it is not yet operational (Le Couteur *et al.*, 2016). The Victorian Parliament Inquiry into Drug Law Reform has further recommended expanding drug courts in Victoria (Parliament of Victoria, 2018). That said, the number of and growth in drug courts in Australia remains small relative to the US, which has witnessed an increase from 458 drug courts in 1998 to 3,100 drug courts in 2017, including at least one in every state (US Department of Justice, 2017).

Key features of the adult drug courts in Australia are outlined in Table 1. As frequently occurs in federal systems, the implementation of drugs courts varies across jurisdictions. Key areas of difference include the timing of the intervention (post-sentence, e.g. New South Wales and Victoria, or pre-sentence, e.g. South Australia and Western Australia), the programme length (6–24 months) and the exclusion criteria (e.g. inclusion or exclusion of offenders charged with violent offences). One further difference is the drug type. The stated criteria for New South Wales, South Australia and Western Australia, as well as for the former Queensland Drug Court, were offenders who were dependent on illicit drugs, while Victoria, the new Queensland Drug Court and the proposed ACT Drug Court include offenders who are dependent on illicit drugs or alcohol.

The Western Australia Drug Court is an exception to the Australian norm as it employs a 'stepped' drug court approach, with a range of programmes targeting different types of offences/offenders from minor to serious. For example, their 2000 model had three programmes: a 'brief intervention regime' (BIR) for those with minor cannabis charges; a 'supervised treatment intervention regime' (STIR) for minor offenders with substance abuse problems; and a 'drug court regime' (DCR) for those who would otherwise likely be imprisoned (Crime Research Centre, 2003). Evaluators ascertained that the programmes were too

Table 1. Key features of adult drug courts in Australia, by jurisdiction.

	NSW	VIC	SA
Date of inception	1999	2002	2000
Eligibility/ offences type	Dependent on the use of prohibited drugs and highly likely to be incarcerated	Dependent on drugs or alcohol, and offender's dependency contributed to the commission of the offence and highly likely to be incarcerated (for up to two years)	Illicit drug dependence (or former dependence with high likelihood of returning to use), and charged with an offence that is related to their drug use, for which they are likely to be incarcerated
Duration of programme	1 year (flexible)	2 years	1 year
Substance	Illicit drugs	Illicit drugs or alcohol	Illicit drugs
Exclusion criteria	Charged with sexual or violent offences or indictable supply of prohibited drugs offences If suffering from a mental condition that could prevent or restrict programme participation	Charged with sexual offence or an offence involving the infliction of actual bodily harm If subject to a Parole Order, Combined Custody and Treatment Order or a Sentencing Order of the County or Supreme Court	Charged with a serious indictable offence If live outside metropolitan boundaries
Phases of programme	3	3	3
Locations/ sites	1 (1999–2010) 2 (2011–2013) 3 (since 2013)	1 (2000–2017) 2 (since 2017)	1 (since 2000)
Court type (see note)	District	Magistrates	Magistrates
Pre- or post-sentence	Post sentence – initial sentence of imprisonment imposed and suspended for duration of programme – final sentence can be less but not more than initial sentence	Post sentence – Drug Treatment Order (DTO) outlining treatment and custodial components with the latter suspended and discharged upon successful completion	Pre-sentence – on bail but offender must plead guilty
Other	All interested applicants are remanded into custody for ≤2 weeks for detoxification and full assessment of individual treatment needs Access to secure, affordable and supported social housing is available for participants with complex needs	Access to short, medium and long term, affordable accommodation and wrap-around support is available for drug court clients that have been identified as homeless or at risk of homelessness	Home detention and electronic monitoring for the first 3 months is mandatory, then night curfew Low cost, furnished rental accommodation is provided for participants and an initial home start pack of household staples is provided as necessary

The Magistrates' Courts and Court of Petty Session are lower courts, the District Court is an intermediate court and the Supreme Court is the highest court (hears the most serious matters).

	QLD (2000–2012)	QLD (2018)	WA
Date of inception	2000	2018	2000
Eligibility/ offences type	Drug dependent and offender's dependency contributed to the commission of the offence and highly likely to be incarcerated for a period of up to four years	Have a severe alcohol or drug substance use disorder that contributed to their offending behaviour and highly likely to be incarcerated for a period of up to four years	Pre-Sentence Order (PSO): experiencing illicit drug related problems and charged with serious offences and facing an immediate and substantial prison sentence Drug Court Regime (DCR): experiencing illicit drug related problems; and charged with less serious offences (sanction that does not include a prison sentence, or a very short prison sentence)
Duration of programme	12 months	2 years	PSO: 6–24 months DCR: 6 months
Substance	Illicit drugs	Illicit drugs or alcohol	Illicit drugs
Exclusion criteria	Charged with sexual offences or offences involving violence against the person, with some exceptions If suffering from any mental condition that could prevent active participation in a rehabilitation programme If subject to a parole order or have served a disqualifying period of imprisonment: > 12 months	Charged with a sexual offence Already serving a term of imprisonment Subject to a parole order	Charged with serious violence, sexual offending or arson
Phases of programme	3	3	1 (DCR) & 3 (PSO)
Locations/ sites	3 (2000–2002) 5 (2002–2012)	1 (since 2018)	1 (since 2000)
Court type (see note)	Magistrates	Magistrates	Court of petty sessions
Pre- or post-sentence	Post sentence – initial sentence of up to four years imprisonment wholly suspended, while offender completed an Intensive Drug Rehabilitation Order (IDRO); progress taken into account on final sentencing	Post sentence – up to four years imprisonment wholly suspended while the offender completes a two-year drug court programme (Drug and Alcohol Treatment Order)	Pre-sentence, i.e. on bail but offender must plead guilty
Other		Accommodation support programmes are available	Rural/regional offenders may participate, provided they are willing to reside in Perth for the duration of the programme All interested offenders will be remanded for 21 or 28 days for assessment

short to meet offender needs (a maximum of six months) (Indermaur and Roberts, 2003). The current version retains a stepped approach but allows a programme of up to 24 months for the most intensive drug court: the 'pre-sentence order' (PSO).

In addition to focusing on principles of therapeutic jurisprudence[1] and providing supervision and monitoring, other general features of the Australian drug court approach include the following.

1. Most drug courts operate for adults only, and provide a pre- or post-sentence option that targets alcohol- or drug-dependent offenders committing serious drug-related offences, using a programme lasting 12 months or more.

2. Consistent with the Australian National Drug Strategy objective of 'harm minimisation' (Commonwealth Department of Health, 2017), most drug courts focus on reducing drug use and drug-related offending rather than complete abstinence or offending cessation. For example, even when the court has stated objectives of abstinence and offending cessation (e.g. the NSW Drug Court), it is acknowledged that this is often not achievable in practice. Significant reductions in drug use and/or offending behaviours are therefore celebrated throughout the drug court programme and rewarded in the final sentencing.

3. All drug courts provide a wide range of treatment options, e.g. detoxification, individual and group counselling, pharmacotherapy (methadone and buprenorphine programmes), residential rehabilitation, residential withdrawal and therapeutic communities.

It is worth noting that youth drug courts have been trialled in some Australian jurisdictions: namely New South Wales, the ACT and Western Australia, albeit without great success (Hughes *et al.*, 2014; Makkai, 2002). For example, a youth drug court was

---

1   Therapeutic jurisprudence is the theoretical framework used for all Australian drug court models. This has not been disputed in Australia, mainly due to the application of the framework as a diversionary measure.

established in New South Wales in November 2001. An evaluation showed that in its first two years, there were 164 referrals to the programme, 75 of whom were found to be eligible (46% of referrals), with 29 (39%) going on to successfully complete the programme (Social Policy Research Centre, 2004). The number of referrals and acceptances were much lower than expected, which curtailed capacity to evaluate programme outcomes. The programme continued until 2012, at which time the government ceased the programme for efficiency and cost reasons: namely, that the programme cost $4 million a year for an average of 17 graduates a year (*Sydney Morning Herald*, 2012). Youth drug courts thus seem to have struggled in Australia due to a lack of referrals, high cost and the general sense that other types of criminal justice diversionary options may be preferable for young Australians.

ROLE OF DRUG COURTS IN AUSTRALIA AND THEIR FIT WITH OTHER DRUG DIVERSION PROGRAMMES

Australia has had a long history of employing criminal justice diversionary responses to drug and drug-related offenders (Hughes, 2009). This is particularly true after 1999, when the Council of Australian Governments' Illicit Drug Diversion Initiative (IDDI) was signed; it committed all states and territories to provide police and court diversion programmes for minor drug offenders, and to refer offenders for education/treatment instead of laying criminal charges (Council of Australian Governments, 1999). Accompanied by considerable federal funding for new drug treatment places (over AU$310 million) (Howard, 1999, 2002), the IDDI resulted in a significant expansion in police and court drug diversion programmes in all states and territories. For example, by 2007 there were 51 different diversion programmes (a threefold increase from 2000) for drug and drug-related offending, targeting different categories of offenders (minor, serious, drug, drug-related) in different stages of the criminal justice process (pre-arrest, pre-trial, pre-sentence, post-sentence) (Hughes and Ritter, 2008).

As such, drug courts in Australia are only one component of the diversionary response for drug and drug-related offenders. The typical set of drug and drug-related diversionary programmes in a state/territory includes four programmes.

- **Police cannabis caution and/or cannabis expiation notice scheme**. A pre-arrest police diversion scheme for use/possession of cannabis that involves either a cannabis caution and referral to a cannabis information and education session or provision of a cannabis expiation notice and requirement to pay a one-off civil penalty (AU$100–AU$300).
- **Police drug diversion**. A pre-arrest police diversion scheme for use/possession of other illicit drugs that leads to a one-off referral to alcohol and other drug assessment, education and/or counselling.
- **Court drug diversion**. A pre-trial court diversion scheme for minor drug and drug-related offenders that provides assessment and 3–4 months of education/treatment, particularly counselling, while offenders are on bail.
- **Drug court**. A pre-sentence or post-sentence programme for serious drug/drug-related offenders that provides therapeutic jurisprudence principles, intensive case management, supervision and compulsory drug treatment for up to 24 months for people who would otherwise be imprisoned (Hughes and Ritter, 2008).

Data from the Australian Alcohol and Other Drug Treatment Services National Minimum Data Set show that in 2012–13 the Australian criminal justice system diverted 24,002 people to alcohol and other drug education or treatment, with police responsible for 48.2% of all diversions to education or treatment (Australian Insitute of Health and Welfare, 2014). In contrast, in 2013 there were an estimated 1,200 people referred to drug courts in Australia, with 570 people being accepted onto drug courts.[2] Moreover, in 2013 in New South Wales specifically, there were a total of 692 referrals to the

---

2   Queensland Drug Courts were not operational in that year.

New South Wales drug courts, 336 people were accepted onto the programme, and 267 participants actively engaged in drug courts (NSW Drug Court, 2014), compared with a total of 2,448 clients who received criminal justice related drug education or treatment for 2012–13 (Australian Institute of Health and Welfare, 2014) and an additional 5,327 offenders who received a cannabis caution (Goh and Holmes, 2014). This illustrates that drug courts service a minority of drug diversion clients in Australia.

That said, drug courts are designed to service the most severe end of the offending spectrum. This is exemplified by considering the typical profile of drug court participants in Australia, who in addition to being drug dependent are often unemployed, have low educational attainment, have multiple prior convictions, and have often served previous sentences of full-time imprisonment prior to their referral to the drug court (Freeman *et al.*, 2000; Payne, 2005).

This role of drug courts in Australia as one part of a broader criminal justice diversionary response is based on several factors. First, the scale of drug and drug-related offending, for which a single intervention such as drug courts would be ill-equipped to cope (Freiberg *et al.*, 2016a). Second, drug courts are highly resource intensive compared with other diversionary programmes (Shanahan *et al.*, 2004, 2017), and sending all offenders through the most costly intervention – drug courts – would be very wasteful (Makkai, 2002). Third, best-practice diversion principles recommend use of a range of programmes with different levels of interventions matched to offender's risk, need and responsivity profiles (ADCA, 1996; Bull, 2005). As such, the Australian diversionary programmes are designed to follow this approach, with less intensive interventions for offenders with lower-level risks and needs and more intensive interventions for offenders with higher-level risks and needs.

LESSONS ON WHAT WORKS

While data is somewhat limited, the existing evidence suggests that Australian drug courts have numerous benefits for participants and society alike, including reducing recidivism and drug use, improvements in health status for participants, a decrease in social problems, and the provision of programmes which are cost-effective. We consider each below.

Recidivism

Most research to date has focused on recidivism. A review of 12 experimental or quasi-experimental impact evaluations of Australian drug courts found that drug courts reduce recidivism more than conventional sanctions. This includes reducing the *incidence* of offending as well as the *frequency* and the *seriousness* of subsequent offending (Kornhauser, 2018). This is further exemplified by three of the most rigorous recidivism studies, from different parts of Australia.

- In 2008, a re-evaluation of the NSW Drug Court that compared reconviction rates among participants in the drug court programme with reconviction rates among a statistically matched comparison group[3] found that those in the drug court group were 37% less likely to be reconvicted of any offence, 65% less likely to be reconvicted of an offence against the person, 35% less likely to be reconvicted of a property offence, and 58% less likely to be reconvicted of a drug offence (Weatherburn *et al.*, 2008).
- An evaluation of recidivism among Queensland Drug Court participants found that after leaving the drug court programme, 59% of those who graduated had been reconvicted of a new offence within two years compared with 77% of those terminated from the programme, and that the average time to first offence was 139 days for those terminated compared with 379 days for graduates (Payne, 2008).

---

3   This was offenders who were deemed eligible for the Drug Court Programme but excluded either because they resided out of the area or because they had been convicted of a violent offence.

- An evaluation of the incidence, frequency and severity of re-apprehension for all SA Drug Court participants over a five-year period (January 2004–December 2008) showed that drug court graduates performed better than non-graduates and a sample of prisoners in terms of reduced incidence of, and longer time to, re-apprehension, but there were no significant differences in terms of the overall frequency of apprehension (Ziersch and Marshall, 2012).

The one exception to these findings comes from the evaluation of the Western Australia Drug Court, which in its early years did not show any tangible reductions in re-offending (Crime Research Centre, 2003). However, this programme was severely criticised for its short six-month programme, with all stakeholders arguing this allowed insufficient time to respond to the needs of the offender. A subsequent review, after the programme length was extended to 24 months, found that the Western Australia Drug Court programme reduced re-offending. This was evidenced by a net reduction in drug-related recidivism of 17% compared with imprisonment and a 10.4% reduction compared with community corrections using a two-year follow up (Department of the Attorney General, 2006).

Drug use

Studies have also shown that participation in drug courts results in reduced use of drugs among those who stay in the programme (Freeman, 2002; Payne, 2005; Social Policy Research Centre, 2004). For example, median weekly spending on illicit drugs reduced from $1,000 per week prior to commencing the programme to $175 per week after four months on the New South Wales programme (Freeman, 2002). In North Queensland, both graduates and non-completers had fewer positive drug tests, indicating a reduction in drug use (Payne, 2005). That said, there have not been any long-term studies monitoring participants after they have completed the programme so there is limited evidence as to whether the benefits are sustained.

Health and social impacts

An evaluation of the NSW Drug Court using prospective follow-up of drug court participants found that participants experienced considerable improvements in health and social functioning within the first four months of being on the programme, and that these improvements were sustained over the 12-month follow-up period (Freeman, 2002). For example, there were improvements in mental health, physical health, general health and reductions in bodily pain. Despite poorer levels of health and well-being than the general population at programme entry, the study found that at the 12-month mark, the mean health scores were either within the normal range for Australian males of the same age or were higher. Similar findings were found in Queensland (Payne, 2005). More generally, as summarised by Freiberg *et al.* (2016a), 'although difficult to quantify' drug courts provide several other health and social benefits to the community, including

> reductions in drug use and associated health issues, easing the burden these offenders place on the health system, the reunification of families, babies born drug-free, the retention of stable accommodation, engagement of offenders in employment, education and training, and a reduction in offending.   (Freiberg *et al.*, 2016a, p. 24)

Cost-effectiveness

Drug courts are often promoted as providing cost savings (Indermaur and Roberts, 2003). Four economic evaluations of Australian drug courts have been conducted to date, each of which has found economic benefits from the drug court evaluated (Department of the Attorney General, 2006; KPMG, 2014; Shanahan *et al.*, 2004). The first was a cost-effectiveness evaluation of the NSW Drug Court conducted over the first two years of the programme (Shanahan *et al.*, 2004). It found that it was marginally more cost-effective in delaying the time to the first offence and in reducing the frequency of offending for those outcome measures selected. There were, however, efficiencies to be gained through, for example, better targeting of the drug court programme (Lind *et al.*, 2002). A second evaluation undertaken in 2008 after significant reforms to the programme estimated that the annual saving due to the NSW Drug Court was AU$1.758 million (the total cost of the programme was AU$16.376 million per annum, compared with AU$18.134 million per annum if they had not participated in the drug court (Goodall *et al.*, 2008)). This shows that well-designed programmes can be cheaper and produce better outcomes than the alternative.

A full economic evaluation was not conducted of the initial Queensland Drug Court, but an analysis of the costs of providing the programme without considering any savings offsets from lower recidivism suggests the drug court was more expensive than imprisonment (Freiberg *et al.*, 2016a). However, it appears that costs not relevant to the drug court itself may have been included in the analysis. Finally, a cost-effectiveness evaluation of the Victoria Drug Court found the drug court to be cost-effective: both less costly than two years in prison and more effective in reducing the frequency and severity of offending (KPMG, 2014).

But it is also clear that, in agreement with international literature on this topic, some drug courts 'work' better than others, and some are cheaper than others. This has led to increased attention on identifying (1) what works for whom, when and why; and (2) barriers and facilitators to good programme and system design.

CHALLENGES FACED IN AUSTRALIAN DRUG COURTS

Implementation challenges have bedevilled most, if not all, Australian drug courts (Crime Research Centre, 2003; Makkai, 2002; Social Policy Research Centre, 2004; Weatherburn *et al.*, 2008). This is exemplified by the SA Drug Court, which imposed a moratorium on any new referrals only seven months post commencement, following an unexpected rate of referrals and acceptances that the court was not equipped to deal with (McRostie and Harrison, 2002). Another common challenge facing Australian drug courts has been low retention rates. For example, the SA Drug Court programme found that only 26.2% of participants completed the programme, with 55.9% terminating before completion and 17.9% voluntarily withdrawing (Skrzypiec, 2006). Most implementation problems have been rectified, as demonstrated by improved outcomes, but as summarised by Makkai and Veraar (2003, p. 10), this indicates that drug courts have seldom been fully efficient or effective from their first day.

Other specific challenges include the following.

Access and equity. Drug courts have tended to be poorly accessed by women and Indigenous offenders. Of note, despite significant overrepresentation of Indigenous offenders in the Australian criminal justice system (Indigenous people are imprisoned at 14.8 times the rate of non-Indigenous people) (Weatherburn, 2014), Indigenous offenders are rarely referred to drug courts. For example, only 7.5–8% of drug court referrals in North Queensland and Western Australia (two areas with significant Indigenous populations) were referred into drug courts (Crime Research Centre, 2003; Payne, 2005). Reasons for this include poor dissemination of programme information to local Indigenous communities and legal practitioners, and problems in establishing rapport with Indigenous offenders at the time of referral (Payne, 2005, p. 11). That said, the major reason for the lack of access is structural and is due to automatic disqualification of any offenders with violent charges (something that is not uncommon among some Indigenous offenders), and a lack of Indigenous-specific treatment facilities in the community. This led the Western Australia evaluators to conclude that 'it may be better to recognize the drug court approach in its current design as mostly suited to a largely white and adult offender group' (Crime Research Centre, 2003, p. vii), and that other types of diversionary options may be better suited for such populations.

Location. Most drug courts have operated in the capital cities. This reflects, in large part, the population distribution in Australia. Those that have expanded to regional areas have illustrated the importance of proximity to treatment, employment and other services as well as clear transport routes if participants are going to be able to attend programmes (Payne, 2005). Such challenges have meant the new Queensland Drug Court was only introduced into Brisbane, and that in Western Australia the court operates in the capital city but is open to people from other areas should they wish to relocate. This differs to the NSW Drug Courts, which are limited to those who live in the immediate surrounding suburbs.

THE IMPORTANCE OF SYSTEM ISSUES IN DRUG COURT DESIGN

Individual drug courts or drug diversion programmes have often been considered in isolation, due to the implicit or explicit assumption that measured effects are, or can be, attributable solely or primarily to the programme. The Australian experiences in using drug courts, and in particular the commonality of implementation issues, have shown that such an approach is problematic. Drug courts are much better conceptualised as operating in a 'complex adaptive system', whereby programme effects and policy interventions will not necessarily be intuitive or controllable only by an individual programme (Checkland, 1981). For example, a drug court by necessity requires input from and the involvement of multiple agencies and sectors. In such an interconnected programme a lack of engagement or delay by any agency in responding to the needs of the offender (or the requirements of the court) can have serious negative implications across the programme, with compounding effects across other agencies (Hughes and Ritter, 2008; Hughes *et al.*, 2014). Two key factors that have been shown in Australia to overcome this and aid in good system design are system mapping and the development of a drug court programme logic (Freiberg *et al.*, 2016a; Hughes *et al.*, 2014; Hughes *et al.*, 2017).

IMPORTANCE OF SYSTEM MAPPING A DRUG COURT

System mapping can help establish all the key stakeholders and services involved in a drug court from the beginning, as well as demonstrate interdependencies and required resources to enable necessary collaborations. It can also help identify where there may be conflicts or potential blockages that are likely to impede effective system functioning. One example of a system map is outlined in Figure 1, which includes the drug court team, the drug treatment system, other social services and special needs populations (e.g. Indigenous offenders in the Australian context) who may require special services for effective participation to occur.

The first and most obvious element of the system is the drug court team. Key questions include whether the correct team of experts has been established, and whether, therefore, all core needs can be met. Here of note, Australian drug courts are increasingly including mental health advisors, housing service providers, cultural advisors and social workers as 'affiliate drug court members' to increase brokerage of such offender needs (Freiberg *et al.*, 2016a; KPMG, 2014). Role clarity for team members is also vital, particularly regarding who will be responsible for case management of the client (justice or health).

Also crucial is the alcohol and other drug (AOD) treatment system. Key questions here are, what treatments are available, what is the quality of the services, and what demand and wait lists already exist? Any drug court introduced into a system that has poor-quality drug treatment options, limited space, long wait lists or insufficient intensity will struggle to perform well, as evidence-based and sustained treatment is vital for long-term change (Freiberg *et al.*, 2016a; Ziersch and Marshall, 2012).

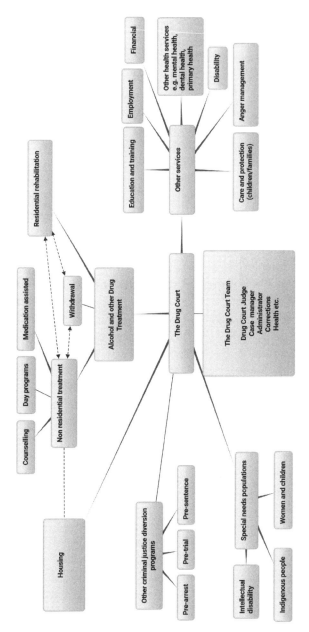

Figure 1. System map for an Australian drug court.

Another consideration in Australia, consistent with best-practice principles of drug treatment provision, is that there is generally an array of treatment options for drug court participants, including residential rehabilitation and non-residential treatment options (Freiberg *et al.*, 2016b). However, this range in turn necessitates clear systems for deciding on the appropriate treatment options for each individual (based on clinical indications, drug type, location, length, setting and modality). Additionally, allowance needs to be made for flows between the AOD treatments, as no single treatment option is likely to be suitable for a given individual for the entire drug court programme. For example, an offender may undergo inpatient withdrawal, followed by a brief period of residential treatment, which is in turn followed by counselling and a day programme. Negotiation to ensure there is the capacity for drug court clients to move between treatment options is required so that treatment progress can be sustained.

The third key element of the system is other social and health services and any other programmes provided within the criminal justice system. For example, while policymakers tend to focus on the drug court team and drug treatment system, it is increasingly clear that attention to other services – particularly housing, financial services and financial counselling, mental health and dental care, employment and education services – are essential to ensure that co-occurring needs can be (swiftly and adequately) met, as failure to do so can lead to delays and drop outs and can reduce long-term benefits (Skrzypiec, 2006; Ziersch and Marshall, 2012). This is one reason that many Australian drug courts now purchase housing for use by drug court clients (see Table 1). Additionally, considering other programmes that are already being provided in the criminal justice system and any potential overlap or conflict with the drug court is necessary for effective and efficient functioning. As an example of overlap having unexpected consequences, an evaluation of the former Queensland Drug Court found that drug court referrals were lower than anticipated following introduction of court-ordered parole (a post-custodial order that included the option to provide AOD treatment) as it was deemed less onerous than the drug court programme (Freiberg *et al.*, 2016a).

Finally, system mapping enables insight into what cross-agency facilitation may be required to ensure quality service provision, communication, monitoring and evaluation, e.g. training, cross-agency agreements (Memorandums of Understanding), new IT systems and/or governance bodies to provide oversight and troubleshoot any cross-agency problems that arise (Freiberg *et al.*, 2016a; National Association of Drug Court Professionals, 2015). Inclusion of such facilitation at the outset may reduce implementation problems or at least increase the capacity for their earlier identification and rectification.

BUILDING A CLEAR PROGRAMME LOGIC FOR A DRUG COURT

Developing a programme logic of a drug court can also aid good system design, by setting out *what* a project will do, *how* it will do it and what needs to be delivered to achieve the desired outcomes (McLaughlin and Jordan, 1999, 2004), and making explicit 'for whom' and 'in what circumstances' a programme works (Pawson, 2006). It helps to build a mutual understanding about programme expectations and to identify any assumptions or flaws in thinking. As such, the use of programme logic has been found particularly useful in criminal justice settings where previously many programmes have been introduced and achieved less-than-desired impacts or even counterproductive impacts (Welsh and Harris, 2016). An example project logic of an Australian drug court is provided in Table 2.[4] The outlined programme logic must:

- Demonstrate the importance of clear targets – here, that the target is high-needs not low-needs offenders – and it must have realistic outcomes so that programmes are not set up to fail. Realistic outcomes are particularly important around goals for

---

4   For another example, see the Queensland Drug Court programme logic published by Freiberg *et al.* (2016b).

Table 2. Example programme logic for an Australian drug court.

Programme objective: To reduce the drug dependency of eligible offenders; to promote the reintegration of eligible offenders into the community; and to promote community safety by reducing the need of drug dependant people to resort to offending behaviour

Problem statement	Inputs: Foundational	Inputs: Programme	Process	Outputs	Short-term outcomes	Medium-term outcomes	Long-term outcomes
There are many seriously AOD dependent people, whose dependency is causing or contributing to offending behavior, and whose AOD-related needs are unable to be met	Legislation, policies & procedures (include cross-agency MOUs and accredited screening and assessment tools) Training IT platform for information sharing Sufficient resources for drug court team, AOD treatment, and brokerage of affiliate services	Detected offenders Court A multi-disciplinary drug court team Screening and assessment AOD treatment (residential and non-residential) Monitoring and testing Sanctions and rewards	Accurate and timely screening and assessment of offender needs Development of a comprehensive and evidence-informed treatment plan matched to offender needs and service capacity Drug court team that establishes a trusted therapeutic relationship with each offender	People who are not eligible e.g. not AOD dependent are excluded early and not pulled into the programme. May be referred to other CJS programmes High-needs AOD dependent offenders who would otherwise be in prison have AOD and other needs met	Holistic, therapeutic and non-adversarial response for AOD dependent offenders Offenders have increased access to AOD treatment and ongoing support Integrated services effectively target co-offending needs of offender	Offenders remain in the programme Stabilisation of AOD dependent offender Stabilisation of offender's non-AOD specific health needs e.g. dental health, mental health, physical health Offenders have increased engagement with training/ literacy/ education and employment	High rate of drug court retention & completion Reduction in severity of AOD dependence Reduction in frequency and severity of offending amongst programme completers, particularly AOD-related offending Reduction in offender risk to community

Table 2. Continued.

Problem statement (continued)	Inputs: Foundational (continued)	Inputs: Programme (continued)	Process (continued)	Outputs (continued)	Short-term outcomes (continued)	Medium-term outcomes (continued)	Long-term outcomes (continued)
	Clear evaluation framework Well-defined governance arrangements with the capacity to oversee and navigate any operational problems that arise	Other services as relevant through brokerage Clear roadmap to monitor, adapt or adjust to issues that arise	Case management & treatment programmes and other programmes delivered as requested Monitoring the offender in community Rapid identification of compliance / non-compliance	Drug court team that functions well and brokers with other agencies Agencies do not feel burdened and are resourced to provide services to drug court clients Court believes drug court is a useful addition	Criminal Justice System (CJS), AOD and related sectors have confidence in the drug court team Offenders risk to the community is managed	Offenders have improved living circumstances, as needed	Harm reduction e.g. reduction in frequency of injury, drug driving & harm violence Integration / reintegration e.g. housing stability, employment & community engagement

Assumptions: That much of the offending is directly attributable to AOD dependence, as opposed to other factors.

That requisite cross-agency MOUs can be established, that will be sufficient resources for all aspects including drug court team, screening, assessment, treatment and brokerage of affiliate services, that drug court team is appropriately staffed by experts, that expert advice particularly clinical assessments about AOD needs and recommended treatment will be adhered to, and that is sufficient flexibility and communication across service delivery system to allow for brokerage/movement across services.

External factors: Current and future demands and gaps in AOD treatment system, housing availability, employment services etc.

reductions in imprisonment as drug courts can only deal with a small number of offenders, so even if they are wholly successful, it is unlikely that they will significantly reduce the number of offenders entering, or staying in, the prison population.

- Highlight the importance of foundational inputs that need to be established for drug court goals to be achieved. Of note is the importance of good and accredited screening and assessment tools so the right people enter the drug court, and scarce resources are not wasted.

- Illustrate the need for a trusting therapeutic relationship to be established by the drug court team with each offender (process), and it must illustrate how, if this occurs, it will increase the probability that offenders will remain in the programme (medium-term outcome) and complete the programme, thereby reducing recidivism (long-term outcome). However, the programme logic also demonstrates that if there are insufficient resources for AOD treatment or brokerage with other services (e.g. housing), then the capacity to meet the needs of the offender will be impinged.

- Show the importance of stability of funding; this is necessary to ensure the programme can be adequately and sustainably implemented with ongoing monitoring and evaluation of programme performance, thus providing information for quality assurance and for programme improvements.

- Demonstrate the importance of staff from health and social systems having confidence in the drug court programme. It is also important to ensure they are not feeling overly burdened. This is one reason that many Australian drug courts cap the number of people in a programme: to ensure offender needs can be properly brokered and met (KPMG, 2014).

CONCLUSION AND IMPLICATIONS

Drug courts in Australia have a long history and continued role in responding to drug-related offending. While there is no 'uniform' drug court in Australia, their emphasis upon targeting adult (not youth) and drug- or alcohol-dependent offenders and their commitment to reducing harm without necessarily achieving abstinence makes them unique. Most important is that the drug courts in Australia are incorporated as part of a broader continuum of drug diversion responses, with drug courts being the last resort in this continuum, reserved for those with the highest level of risk and needs.

The evidence base on Australian drug courts has shown that drug courts can reduce offending and drug use, improve social functioning and reduce costs to society. But it also demonstrates that not all drug courts have been equally effective, and hence good programme and system design is vital to reduce implementation challenges or avoid programme failure. Key lessons for facilitating good programme and system design are, first, being realistic about in what contexts, and for whom, drug courts work. For example, they may work better in larger cities, where services are well located and good transport routes exist, but work less well in poorly resourced regional areas, where distance is a major obstacle. Second is the importance of considering the system and system operations (something that can be aided by system mapping and programme logic models) to: (1) ensure all relevant stakeholders and agencies are involved from the outset; (2) identify, and where possible address, potential blockages (e.g. wait lists for treatment); (3) put in place systems for cross-agency relationships, e.g. IT systems and governance bodies; and (4) ensure that programmes are adequately resourced such that all needs of the offenders can be met.

Finally, we highlight that drug courts, at least when implemented as per the Australian model, are not 'cheap', and that to be effective they must be well-funded and supported by multiple agencies. This is why Australia has realised that drug courts are not the only 'answer', and that the best systems employ drug courts as part of a broader platform of criminal justice system responses to drugs and drug-related offending.

REFERENCES

ADCA (1996). Best practice in the diversion of alcohol and other drug offenders. In *Proceedings of the ADCA Diversion Forum*. Alcohol and Other Drugs Council of Australia, Canberra.

Australian Institute of Health and Welfare (2014). Alcohol and other drug treatment and diversion from the Australian criminal-justice system 2012–13. *Bulletin 125*. Australian Insitute of Health and Welfare, Canberra.

Bull, M. (2005). A comparative review of best practice guidelines for the diversion of drug related offenders. *International Journal of Drug Policy* 16, 223–234.

Checkland, P. (1981). *Systems Thinking, Systems Practice (Includes a 30-Year Retrospective)*. John Wiley.

Commonwealth Department of Health (2017). National drug strategy 2017–2026. Commonwealth Department of Health, Canberra.

Council of Australian Governments (1999). Tough on drugs! Diversion programme. COAG, Canberra.

Crime Research Centre (2003). Evaluation of the Perth drug court pilot project: final report. University of Western Australia, Perth.

Department of the Attorney General (2006). A review of the Perth drug court. Department of the Attorney General, Perth.

Freeman, K. (2002). New South Wales drug court evaluation: health, well-being and participant satisfaction. NSW Bureau of Crime Statistics and Research, Sydney.

Freeman, K. (2003). Evaluating Australia's first drug court: research challenges. Paper presented at the *Evaluation in Crime and Justice: Trends and Methods Conference, Canberra*.

Freeman, K., and Donnelly, N. (2005). Early-phase predictors of subsequent program compliance and offending among NSW Adult Drug Court participants. *Contemporary Issues in Crime and Justice*, Number 88. NSW Bureau of Crime Statistics and Research, Sydney.

Freeman, K., Lawrence Karski, R., and Doak, P. (2000). New South Wales drug court evaluation: program and participant profiles. NSW Bureau of Crime Statistics and Research, Sydney.

Freiberg, A., Payne, J., Gelb, K., Morgan, A., and Makkai, T. (2016a). Queensland drug and specialist courts review: a final report. Queensland Courts, Brisbane.

Freiberg, A., Payne, J., Gelb, K., Morgan, A., and Makkai, T. (2016b). Queensland drug and specialist courts review: Appendix G – Drug court program logic. Queensland Courts, Brisbane.

Goh, D., and Holmes, J. (2014). New South Wales recorded crime statistics 2013. NSW Bureau of Crime Statistics and Research, Sydney.

Goodall, S., Norman, R., and Haas, M. (2008). The costs of NSW Drug Court. *Contemporary Issues in Crime and Justice*, Number 122. NSW Bureau of Crime Statistics and Research, Sydney:.

Howard, J. (1999). Media release: tough on drugs diversion program. Office of the Prime Minister, Canberra.

Howard, J. (2002). Media release: illicit drug diversion initiative. Office of the Prime Minister, Canberra.

Hughes, C., and Ritter, A. (2008). *A Summary of Diversion Programs for Drug and Drug-Related Offenders in Australia*. DPMP Monograph Series, No. 16. National Drug and Alcohol Research Centre, Sydney.

Hughes, C., Shanahan, M., Ritter, A., McDonald, D., and Gray-Weale, F. (2014). *Evaluation of Australian Capital Territory Drug Diversion Programs*. DPMP Monograph Series, No. 25. National Drug and Alcohol Research Centre, Sydney.

Hughes, C., Shanahan, M., Sotade, O., and Ritter, A. (2017). Towards a new ACT Drug and Alcohol Court: a program and systems perspective. Drug Policy Modelling Program, NDARC, UNSW, Sydney.

Hughes, C. E. (2009). Capitalising upon political opportunities to reform drug policy: a case study into the development of the Australian 'Tough on Drugs–Illicit Drug Diversion Initiative'. *International Journal of Drug Policy* 20(5), 431–437.

Indermaur, D., and Roberts, L. (2003). Drug courts in Australia: the first generation. *Current Issues in Criminal Justice* 15, 136–154.

Jones, C. (2011). Intensive judicial supervision and drug court outcomes: interim findings from a randomised controlled trial. *Contemporary Issues in Crime and Justice*, No. 152. NSW Bureau of Crime Statistics and Research, Sydney.

Jones, C. G. A., and Kemp, R. I. (2014). The strength of the participant–judge relationship predicts better drug court outcomes. *Psychiatry, Psychology and Law* 21(2), 165–175.

Kornhauser, R. (2018). The effectiveness of Australia's drug courts. *Australian & New Zealand Journal of Criminology* 51(1), 76–98.

KPMG (2014). Evaluation of the Drug Court of Victoria: final report. KPMG, Melbourne.

Le Couteur, C., Rattenbury, S., and Barr, A. (2016). Parliamentary Agreement for the 9th Legislative Assembly. Chief Minister Treasury and Economic Development Directorate, Canberra.

Lind, B., Weatherburn, D., Chen, S., Shanahan, M., Lancsar, E., Haas, M., and De Abreu Lourenco, R. (2002). New South Wales drug court evaluation: cost-effectiveness. NSW Bureau of Crime Statistics and Research, Sydney.

Makkai, T. (2002). The emergence of drug treatment courts in Australia. *Substance Use & Misuse* 37(12–13), 1567–1594.

Makkai, T., and Veraar, K. (2003). Final report on the South East Queensland Drug Court. *Technical and Background Paper Series*, No. 6. Australian Institute of Criminology, Canberra.

McLaughlin, J. A., and Jordan, G. B. (1999). Logic models: a tool for telling your program's performance story. *Evaluation and Program Planning* 22(1), 65–72.

McLaughlin, J. A., and Jordan, G. B. (2004). Using logic models. In *Handbook of Practical Program Evaluation*, Volume 2, pp. 7–32. John Wiley.

McRostie, H., and Harrison, A. (2002). Evaluation of the drug court pilot program: interim report. Office of Crime Statistics and Research, Adelaide.

National Association of Drug Court Professionals (2015). *Adult Drug Court Best Practice Standards*, Volume 2. National Association of Drug Court Professionals, Virginia.

NSW Government (1998). Drug Court Act 1998. NSW, Sydney.

NSW Drug Court (2014). 2013 annual review. NSW Drug Court, Parramatta.

NSW Drug Court (2016). 2016 annual review. NSW Drug Court, Parramatta.

NSW Drug Court (2018). NSW Drug Court website (http://www.drug-court.justice.nsw.gov.au/).

Parliament of Victoria (2018). Inquiry into drug law reform. Parliament of Victoria – Law Reform Road and Community Safety Committee, Melbourne.

Pawson, R. (2006). *Evidence-Based Policy: A Realist Perspective*. SAGE, London.

Payne, J. (2005). Final report of the North Queensland Drug Court evaluation. *Technical and Background Paper Series*, No. 17. Australian Institute of Criminology, Canberra.

Payne, J. (2006). Specialty courts: current issues and future prospects. *Trends & Issues in Crime & Criminal Justice*, No. 217. Australian Institute of Criminology, Canberra.

Payne, J. (2008). The Queensland Drug Court: a recidivism study of the first 100 graduates. Australian Institute of Criminology, Canberra.

Queensland Courts (2018). Queensland Drug and Alcohol Court (http://www.courts.QLD.gov.au/courts/drug-court, retrieved 15 February 2018).

Shanahan, M., Lancsar, E., Haas, M., Lind, B., Weatherburn, D., and Chen, S. (2004). Cost-effectiveness analysis of the New South Wales adult drug court program. *Evaluation Review* 28(1), 3–27.

Shanahan, M., Hughes, C., and McSweeney, T. (2017). Australian police diversion for cannabis offences: assessing program outcomes and cost-effectiveness. Monograph No. 66. National Drug Law Enforcement Research Fund, Canberra.

Shaw, J., and Smith, J. (2001). Legislative comment – Choosing life: the drug summit and beyond. *Macquarie Law Journal* 1(1), 145–171.

Skrzypiec, G. (2006). The South Australian Drug Court: an analysis of participant retention rates. South Australian Office of Crime Statistics and Research, Adelaide.

Social Policy Research Centre (2004). Evaluation of the NSW Youth Drug and Alcohol Court Program: final report. NSW Attorney-General's Department, Sydney.

Sydney Morning Herald (2012). Quiet death of the youth drug court. *Sydney Morning Herald*, 9 July (retrieved from https://www.smh.com.au/politics/federal/quiet-death-of-the-youth-drug-court-20120708-21p7h.html).

Taplin, S. (2002). New South Wales drug court evaluation: a process evaluation. NSW Bureau of Crime Statistics and Research, Sydney.

US Department of Justice (2017). Drug court. National Criminal Justice Reference Service, Rockville.

Weatherburn, D. (2014). The problem of Indigenous over-representation in prison. In *Arresting Incarceration: Pathways out of Indigenous Imprisonment*, Volume 1. Aboriginal Studies Press.

Weatherburn, D., Jones, C., Snowball, L., and Hua, J. (2008). The NSW Drug Court: a re-evaluation of its effectiveness. *Contemporary Issues in Crime and Justice*, No. 121. NSW Bureau of Crime Statistics and Research, Sydney.

Welsh, W. N., and Harris, P. W. (2016). *Criminal Justice Policy and Planning: Planned Change*. Routledge, New York.

Ziersch, E., and Marshall, J. (2012). The South Australian Drug Court: a recidivism study. Office of Crime Statistics and Research, Adelaide.

CHAPTER 3

The Irish Experience: Policy Transfer from US Drug Courts

By John Collins

Ireland is undergoing a significant shift in its national response to drug issues. As the Taoiseach (Prime Minister) wrote in the foreword to the 2017–23 National Drug Strategy, '[f]or the ideal of a Republic of Opportunity to be meaningful, it must apply to all. Treating substance abuse and drug addiction as a public health issue, rather than as a criminal justice issue, helps individuals, helps families, and helps communities' (Department of Health, 2017, p. 3). Within this context significant questions about the use of criminal sanctions as a supposed deterrence for drug consumption have been well raised (*Hot Press Magazine*, 2018). As one discussant in a joint university-service provider townhall on criminalisation in June 2018 argued,

> This is not about decriminalising drugs, this is about decriminalising people who use drugs. When somebody is using drugs, branding them as a criminal isn't helpful – it just drives them further away, and makes them feel stigmatised, isolated and apart. Instead, we need to be pulling people closer, focusing on their health and helping people live the best and healthiest lives they can lead.
>
> (*Hot Press Magazine*, 2018)

The above refers specifically to the criminalisation of consumption practices and individuals who engage in them. However, within this context interventions that purport to offer a more 'health'- or 'treatment'-oriented approach to dealing with drug-involved offenders come under greater scrutiny. As a society shifts away from a belief in the power of criminalisation to deter or manage drug use, how does an intervention based on the premise of court-imposed treatment, with deeply questionable efficacy, stand up? As Hunt and Stevens argued in 2004 with regard to UK drug policy, the public health–harm reduction approach 'may be diluted and even undermined by the shift to coercion', adding that 'harm reduction fails adequately to resolve an inherent tension that enables both coercive measures to reduce crime and others that seek primarily to improve individual health' (Hunt and Stevens, 2004, p. 337).

This chapter is intended as a broad critical literature and policy review, drawing in particular on key scholars who have undertaken qualitative assessments of the Dublin Drug Treatment Court (DDTC) and the international context of its implementation. It will juxtapose these with a re-examination of government evaluations of the DDTC, virtually all of which have portrayed a policy intervention that is simultaneously politically popular and yet operationally problematic, particularly struggling to attract and retain clients. The chapter will also provide a critical review of the constitutional position of the DDTC and suggest that the current operation poses serious due-process concerns.

THE ORIGINS OF THE DUBLIN
DRUG TREATMENT COURT

The Irish drug court experiment emerged during an era when drugs and drug market related crime, particularly the murder of journalist Veronica Guerin, received significant public attention (Loughran et al., 2015). This coincided with increased recognition that the criminal justice system was failing to manage the broader issues of treatment and public health associated with problematic use (Loughran and McCann, 2006). For example, one study in the early 2000s alarmedly estimated that 80% of 'indictable crime' in Dublin was drug related (Farrell, 2002, p. 11). While specific public health interventions, for example methadone, were clearly shown to reduce drug-related crime, there remained a broad reticence to embark on a more pronounced shift towards a public health policy orientation (Loughran and McCann, 2006).

Tough-on-crime policies, such as mandatory minimum sentences, became increasingly popular. Drug courts, meanwhile, emerged as 'the only liberal-seeming initiative' of the new government that came to power in 1997 (Butler, 2013, p. 6). As Fianna Fáil leader Bertie Ahern stated at the time,

> Fianna Fáil in government /.../ for the first time, will link rehabilitated addicts to job training and placement. By introducing a drug court programme, we will use the justice system in an imaginative way to rehabilitate addicts charged with non-violent offences and reduce the prison revolving door for drug addicts.   (Ahern, 1997)

Meanwhile, during the 1990s, methadone provision expanded in a delicate and low-key manner (Butler, 2002). Indeed Fianna Fáil's attitude to methadone expansion at the time, in many ways ideologically closer to the United States's (US) abstinence orientation, grudgingly accepted that methadone could be part of 'the detoxification and rehabilitation of addicts' but that it would only play a 'secondary role' (Butler, 2002, p. 8). This typified the ambivalent and divergent strands within Irish drug policy at the time. It was witnessing a technocratic trend towards harm-reduction-oriented treatment modalities, while government policies and rhetoric tended towards more populist, tough-on-crime, approaches. At best, the latter were ostensibly moderated by 'criminal justice-lite' alternatives such as drug courts.

In this sense Ireland could perhaps be seen as overtly and ideologically aspiring towards a US approach to the War on Drugs while quietly and technocratically moving towards a system based on European-style harm reduction. The latter won out on methadone, and one year after Fianna Fáil had produced its position paper that was openly sceptical of methadone, the Minister for Health and Children in a Fianna Fáil majority government signed a new protocol for prescribing methadone into law, representing what Butler describes as 'the most important policy proposals in the 30 year history of drug treatment in Ireland' (Butler, 2002, p. 9). Within this broader context of divergent public discourses and obscured policy changes, the DDTC Pilot emerged as an unquestionable US import, somewhat adapted to Irish circumstances (Nolan, 2009).

THE AMERICAN ORIGINS OF THE DUBLIN DRUG COURT

In October 1997, under the initiative of the Fianna Fáil government, the Working Group on a Courts Commission began a study of US drug court models. It was chaired by Supreme Court Judge Susan Denham, along with five other judges (Working Group on a Courts Commission, 1998). It was subsequently criticised for having no representation from the Irish healthcare sector and for a broader failure to look beyond the criminal justice sector (Butler et al., 2000). The Working Group drew heavily on US experiences and convened a conference on the issue, inviting experts from US drug courts.

Further, Judge Gerard Haughton, who would go on to become Ireland's first drug court judge, visited a drug court in California as well as ones in Australia, while another judge visited Toronto, and various members of the Working Group and the judiciary visited conferences of the National Association of Drug Court Professionals (NADCP) in the US (Nolan, 2009). This again produced criticism that the report implicitly and explicitly adopted US biases and rhetoric towards a War on Drugs model that was alien to the setting it was being evaluated for. Further, the report was criticised for implicitly suggesting that the treatment sector should be subservient to the criminal justice sector in the operation of the drug court (Butler et al., 2000).

The work of Butler (2013) highlights that the importation of the drug court model to Ireland was not demand-driven. He quotes one judge as saying that while there was no active 'resistance' from the judiciary,

There was this view that drug courts were unnecessary, that judges were using the Probation Service and the local drug treatment agencies insofar as they existed. And whether a more kind of concentrated intervention was necessary? Well we were persuaded at some point that drug courts had /.../ better outcomes.

(Quoted in Butler 2013, p. 9)

As one consultant psychiatrist argued, the creation of the drug court was seen as 'politically driven', meaning that Ireland 'adopted the American model, hook, line and sinker, to the extent that we can' (quoted in Butler, 2013, p. 9). Other civil servants interviewed proffered an even greater level of scepticism, suggesting some of the judiciary's reticence stemmed from a sense of 'why should one court be called a drug court when every court is a drug court in effect?' The answer, this same civil servant suggested, was that it was 'badged and promoted as a brave new world' (quoted in Butler, 2013, p. 9).

Butler's qualitative analysis suggests an externally generated model being imposed in an environment where many of the tenets were already being implemented and negotiated between the court system and treatment services. He quotes one consultant psychiatrist at length:

I saw a lot of frustrated justices who I've got to know over the years /.../ who would have preferred a slightly beefed up Probation Service; and who are well capable of handling these things, and in fact probably didn't need a bloody [specialist drug] court /.../ to do it, [judges] who would take good court reports, where there was integrated care between [the] health service, the Probation Service; and mandated treatment and supervision orders that would allow for people to get the treatment they required, without /.../ this very expensive, specialist system.   (Quoted in Butler, 2013, p. 9)

This perceived lack of consultative breadth and institutional buy-in among key stakeholders arguably established many of the fault lines that would hinder the DDTC's development. For example, almost two decades after the Working Group first met, the DDTC continued to struggle to fill key roles such as a dedicated treatment counsellor or social welfare officer (Loughran *et al.*, 2015). Other external observers viewed the Working Group process as a model of consultation and an example of the 'careful and deliberative manner in which the Irish planned their drug court' (Nolan, 2009, p. 111). In the context of US experts and judges descending on Irish conferences and encouraging Irish officials to 'JUST DO IT!' (Working Group on a Courts Commission, 1998, p. 101), the subsequent delays could be read as an example of careful deliberation (Bean, 2002). Others view it as an example of unplanned policy delay which resulted in another three years before the DDTC began.

Butler again offers the most compelling explanation: it was, he suggests, delayed by an unplanned, multifaceted and indeterminate convergence of forces. Evidencing this, one of the judges involved in the process could not explain the delay, thereby mitigating the idea of a conscious protraction (Butler, 2013). Others plausibly suggested that delays inevitably arose from complex interest group and institutional politics that required a negotiation of division of labour among key stakeholders (Butler, 2013). Unlike US drug courts, which emerged into an almost complete policy vacuum in many cases, the DDTC was created within a system with well-defined and hard-fought institutional battle lines. Butler uses this point to highlight the fundamental weakness of the drug court idea in Ireland, its running afoul of and exacerbating 'tensions between healthcare and criminal justice systems' (Butler, 2013, p. 10; Butler *et al.*, 2000). As one consultant psychiatrist interviewed highlighted,

> that may have been – the real resistance /.../ a lack of good debate in the initial stages, that someone had gone away, seen the concept, transplanted it into the Irish situation, and that the transplant was rejected.   (Quoted in Butler, 2013, p. 10)

Another, this time a probation manager, highlighted a lack of deeper evaluation of the cultural and ideological implications of importing the model early on:

I think from what I've seen of it that it was set up in a fairly pragmatic, political with a small 'p' kind of approach: 'let's introduce
this system here'. I think a lot of the underlying issues, including
the underlying philosophy, weren't really examined very closely.

(Quoted in Butler, 2013, p. 10)

These underlying issues, as Butler suggests, remained as 'unresolved tensions which continued to have a negative impact on the
ongoing delivery of the drug court model' (Butler, 2013, p. 10). In
this sense the weaknesses of the Irish drug court model were not simple technocratic or implementation-related issues. They were instead
fundamental institutional, ideological and political issues baked into
the model from the outset that largely explain why it was 'rejected'
by the broader system.

BUILDING THE PILOT

In 1998 the Working Group published a report recommending the
implementation of drug courts, writing that

Drug Courts are not a panacea, they are not a universal remedy
for the drug problem. However, they have the potential to be an
effective part of a pattern of projects and activities to heal the drug
problem and the social evils it creates in society.

(Working Group on a Courts Commission, 1998, p. 13)

Interestingly, the working group diverged from the US vision,
which rejected methadone and maintenance in favour of abstinence.[1]
Instead, the Working Group argued that 'while total abstinence is
the optimal object of a drugs treatment programme the alternative
system of methadone maintenance should not be excluded' (quoted

---

1   In recent years US drug courts have shifted towards a greater acceptance of
     medication assistance as treatment (Department of Health and Human Ser-
     vices, 2015).

in Butler *et al.*, 2000, p. 55). Within this grudging acceptance can be found a partial explanation for subsequent failure. Firstly, a group made up largely of criminal justice experts were already passing judgement on treatment modalities within the drug court, something anathema to basic understandings of public health (Csete and Wolfe, 2017). Secondly, the court was limiting itself to an unachievable vision of abstinence through court-mandated treatment, instead of deferring to the health sector and service providers on the key needs of clients. The court established itself as grudgingly accepting of principles of treatment that were soon to become a bedrock of the Irish heroin response. Instead, the DDTC model was largely crafted based on US principles that would become less and less relevant over the coming decades.

Based on the Working Group's report, the Irish Minister for Justice, John O'Donoghue, established the Drug Court Planning Committee with two dozen representatives from across government departments and agencies. After six months of, by some accounts heated, discussion, the planning committee produced a 'working compromise' that suggested the creation of a smaller steering committee that could focus on 'actual implementation of the pilot', which was to run for 18 months, although the Steering Committee eventually shortened that to a little over 12 months (Drug Court Planning Committee, 1999; quoted in Nolan, 2009, p. 111).

The first participant was referred to the DDTC on 16 January 2001, representing the inauguration of the pilot and evaluation stage, which would run until 31 January 2002. The DDTC aimed at offenders over the age of 18 who had already pleaded guilty to 'non-violent, drug-related, criminal offences at district court level and who were liable to receive a custodial sentence' (Butler, 2013, p. 7). Participants were to undergo three phases, bronze, silver and gold, lasting up to two years, with a mixture of treatment and education overseen by the drug court team under the leadership of a judge (Butler, 2013). To 'graduate' required abstinence from illegal drug taking as well as no further law breaking. Participants who did not progress were 'terminated' and returned to their original court facing a possible prison sentence (Butler, 2013).

At the end of the pilot an independent evaluation was carried out by Michael Farrell. He suggested the court faced three options.

1. 'Discontinue', an option he rejected as having 'no reason to' recommend especially in light of 'the considerable energy that has been expended on developing and implementing the Programme' (Farrell, 2002, p. 9).
2. 'Immediate mainstreaming', Farrell professed to favour this but pointed to the significant institutional and planning hurdles that would need to be overcome 'as well as a number of high level issues identified in this report' (Farrell, 2002, p. 9).
3. The preferred option, 'a dual strategy over the next 12–18 months' based on 'Continuation and Expansion of the Pilot and Development of a Drug Court Planning Programme'. Or to put the 'emphasis /.../ on the research and development activity necessary to roll-out the Drug Court more widely while at the same time continuing and expanding the current pilot to further test and refine the emerging model' (Farrell, 2002, p. 9).

One of the professed reasons for its hedged recommendations was its methodological limitations. Firstly, given the proximity of the review to the entry of the first client – a little over 12 months – it was impossible to evaluate the impact of the court on recidivism and relapse (Farrell, 2002). The former represents perhaps the one area where international evaluations of drug courts have shown generally positive although contested outcomes (Sevigny *et al.*, 2013). Further, the sample size was recognised to be too small to allow 'reliable conclusions' about the criteria examined (Farrell, 2002).

As a 2011 evaluation by the non-partisan US Government Accountability Office (GAO) found, less than 20% of studies cited to support drug court outcomes actually used sound social science principles (US Government Accountability Office, 2011). Further, the US Congressional Research Service highlighted a major issue around the lack of control groups from whom the outcomes of drug court participants could be judged against (Franco, 2010). The Farrell study highlighted a similar problem for Ireland:

> Regrettably there is no single source of data available on the full range of variables which ideally should be collated for a Control Group. Ultimately, An Garda Síochána and the Courts Service provided information on the offending behaviour of a group of known drug misusing offenders resident in the South Inner City /.../ Because the drug use and treatment status of this group is not known they are not a suitable control – the information is provided here merely as an indication of the offending patterns of a group of offenders broadly similar to those participating in the Drug Court.
>
> (Farrell, 2002, p. 14)

Similar issues militated against a reasonable cost-effectiveness assessment of the drug court. These were compounded by an inability to assess 'accurate costs of all of the services involved' (Farrell, 2002, p. 88). Despite an overt goal of reducing the number of nights spent in prison by participants – an experience not borne out by meta-analyses of US drug courts, which have found no impact on overall incarceration (Sevigny et al., 2013) – the report concluded that 'the early indication is that over the pilot period the Drug Court did not effect significant cost savings to the justice system' (Farrell, 2002, pp. 92–94).

To summarise, the Dublin Drug Court Pilot was evaluated on too short a timeline to get a clear sense of actual impacts on clients, had too few participants to make any reasonable generalisations about the group, and lacked a control group against which participant outcomes could be evaluated. In this context, perhaps the best that could be argued at the point of evaluation was that the court was aimed at a population who could benefit from an alternative to repeat incarceration, but it could not make any reliable claims that the drug court achieved this.

Nevertheless, based on what could be termed a 'principle of optimal possibilities', where the court was viewed in terms of its possible outcomes, combined with a recognition of sunk costs, the study recommended its continuation. The DDTC, despite poor initial results, was to continue.

THERAPEUTIC JUSTICE – IGNORING
PHILOSOPHICAL DIVERGENCE

From the outset, the DDTC was developed with pragmatism in mind, thereby eschewing the broader therapeutic justice and deep abstinence ideologies of other drug court models (Nolan, 2009). Ultimately, however, scholars have suggested this may have simply served to paper over fundamental issues of adapting models developed in different legal, socioeconomic and cultural contexts. As Nolan writes, 'adjustments made to the legal programs are not the end of the story. The programs themselves also effect change in the legal culture to which they have been transferred' (Nolan, 2009, p. 40). Nolan cites one legal scholar, Gunther Teubner, to highlight the point:

> When a foreign rule is imposed on a domestic culture, I submit, something else is happening. It is not transplanted into another organism, rather it works as a fundamental irritation which triggers a whole series of unexpected events.   (Teubner, 2001, p. 418)

International comparative studies have highlighted the centrality of 'therapeutic justice' (TJ) ideas to drug courts, ultimately representing their philosophical and normative basis (Stolle *et al.*, 2000). TJ has been described as a 'comprehensive law movement' that identifies the perceived weaknesses of the criminal justice system in responding to key social issues and thereby strives for a 'more humane, therapeutic, beneficial, humanistic, healing, restorative, curative, collaborative, and comprehensive' approach (Daicoff, 2000, p. 465).

TJ ideas developed in response to the revolving door of prisons during the peak of the US War on Drugs of the 1980s and 1990s. Many argue that, to be effective and 'authentic', drug courts should remain closely tethered to this original underlying philosophy (Jones and Kawalek, 2018). Nevertheless, international jurisdictions have been mixed in the extent to which they embrace, debate or simply ignore the principles, practical concerns and philosophical issues posed by drug courts and the TJ movement (Nolan, 2009). For example, in the US, the idea of TJ is hardly contested, receiving widespread and enthusiastic support among the many thousand drug court professionals throughout the country (Stolle *et al.*, 2000).

In Australia, the concept has been hotly debated and at times contested, but ultimately accepted under the balancing view that jurists must adopt extreme caution in implementing TJ initiatives out of a risk of abuse of power (King, 2008; Nolan, 2009). Similarly, in Canada, although the term has been largely accepted, the judiciary has shown significant reserve in implementation of sanctioning under TJ procedures (Nolan, 2009). In Ireland and Scotland, viewed as perhaps the closest cousins in their adaptations of the drug courts, one finds a common rejection or lack of awareness of TJ as a philosophy. However, the two diverge over the reasons for their rejection of the TJ philosophy. Scotland arguably eschews TJ out of a desire to maintain strict adherence to due-process principles and the role of the judiciary as an impartial arbiter of these (see Chapter 1). Ireland, on the other hand, showing perhaps more flexibility in the application of due process in the context of drug courts, appears to reject TJ more for reasons of expedience. Further, in the Irish case there is perhaps an element of cultural exceptionalism from the US and not wanting to be seen as adopting US practice too directly (Butler, 2013; Nolan, 2009).

The general rejection of TJ runs contrary to the advice from Judge Patrick Morris, of California, to the Irish Working Group,

> Select your first Drug Court judge with great care. Most critically, this judge must philosophically "buy-into" the idea of restorative justice; that is, hold a belief that it is possible to "rehabilitate" and "reintegrate" offenders in a way that they are able to live freely and responsibly in a community. He or she must be willing to learn about the compulsive and relapsing nature of drug addiction and the limitations of judicial coercion as a drug rehabilitation tool /.../ It is important that this judge be willing to leave the bench and

THE IRISH EXPERIENCE 63

enter the community in order to educate and build public support
for this new model of jurisprudence.
(Quoted in Working Group on a Courts Commission, 1998, p. 99)

As Butler's interviewees highlighted, Ireland has retained a general
disinterest, bordering on distrust, for the ideas of TJ. While all
acknowledge the drug court produced an altered, more 'hands-on'
interaction between judges and clients, most dismissed or were
unaware of the theoretical framework justifying it. As one judge
argued, 'we're not therapists. We don't have the training and it
would be foolish of us to take on that role' (quoted in Butler, 2013,
p. 9). Other analyses have portrayed the Irish rejection as a more
consciously pragmatic neglect (Bean, 2002; Nolan, 2009).

THE LEGISLATIVE AND CONSTITUTIONAL
LIMITATIONS OF THE DRUG COURT

Ireland, unlike Scotland, has rejected the TJ approach as lacking
resonance with its cultural and legal systems but has simultaneously
adopted a more flexible attitude to the legal rights of drug court
clients (Nolan, 2009). This flexibility developed from the expediency
of establishing the court under existing legislation, whereby it operates under a post-plea/conviction bail bond system, where clients are
released on bail in lieu of a custodial sentence. The bail can thus be
revoked as a sanctioning process (Nolan, 2009). The constitutional,
due-process and international legal ramifications of this expediency
approach were highlighted early on by the first Irish Drug Court
Judge, Judge Gerard Haughton:

> I was quite direct in informing the lawyers that I did not see any
> particular role for them in appearing on a regular basis in the court
> and that on occasions defendants' bail may be revoked for a short
> period. Again, quite directly I conceded that such bail revocation
> orders could almost certainly be successfully challenged in the High
> Court. The result of such a challenge would be a fairly substantial

fee earned from the State, the release of the client and his termination from the Drug Court Programme, none of which was of
any long-term benefit to him. This has been accepted and once a
participant is accepted in our Drug Court the lawyers (who do have
a right to appear) step aside.   (Quoted in Nolan, 2009, p. 128)

The constitutional problems with this approach are readily apparent. Further, as Bean writes, 'it may satisfy those who see rehabilitation as the goal' but it 'reawakens also other criticisms of rehabilitation made in the 1960s, namely that it gives unbridled power to those
intent on rehabilitating the offender' (Bean, 2002, p. 1610). Other
concerns around due process were highlighted in Nolan's study. One
judge professed discomfort with the lack of due process within the
system, the risk of abuses and of an expanded scope for a judge to
personally interfere in the life choices of a client in ways that would
traditionally be perceived as far outside the legitimate scope of the
judiciary (Nolan, 2009). The judge in question pointed to one case
where a client was sanctioned with seven days in custody for alleged
shoplifting and general non-compliance. The judge highlighted that
based on the merits, the client would likely have 'gotten off' under
a more typical court hearing for the charge. In another case, the
judge was encouraged to press a client to take contraception in the
wake of a number of miscarriages. The judge refused, highlighting
it as an inappropriate personal issue for a member of the judiciary
to comment on, conveying a sense of legal imperative as they do
(Nolan, 2009, p. 130).

Farrell's 2002 evaluation found that '[one] third of the participants have had their bail revoked by the Drug Court Judge during
their time on the Programme, ranging from a minimum of 2 days to
a maximum of 40 days' (Farrell, 2002, p. 79). In light of due-process
issues and the conspicuous absence of defence lawyers, this poses
serious concerns. It often results in clients being penalised for infractions at a much lower burden of proof than would be applied in a
typical court setting (Nolan, 2009). Another issue centres on cases
where judges are enabled to make decisions based on pre-court meet-
ings without hearing from the defendants (Nolan, 2009).

This is in contrast to the Scottish drug court, where 'the legitimate role of the defense agent does not change in the drug court and includes that of advocacy, representing the interest of the client and safeguarding the rights of the defendant' (Fife Drug Court, 2002, p. 9). Scotland explicitly rejected the Irish approach as a breach of clients' due-process rights and the European Convention on Human Rights. On the latter point they believed it would represent a breach of a right of decisions 'adverse to the offender' to be 'aired in open court' (Nolan, 2009, p. 129). As Nolan writes,

> Scottish sheriffs did not originally have the authority to impose a short-term jail sentence; they lacked the statutory authority to do so. When the Scottish Parliament eventually gave them this power, sheriffs were still very reluctant to use it.   (Nolan, 2009, p. 129)

A NEAR-DEATH EXPERIENCE, 2005–2009

The Dublin Pilot, from the outset, witnessed a phenomenon similar to other international examples: poor or questionable outcomes masked by deep political popularity. From the outset, the 2002 Farrell Report acknowledged low participation and a lack of cost-effectiveness but remained optimistic about the possibility to resolve the 'teething problems' (Butler, 2013, p. 7; Farrell, 2002). In 2005, the Courts Service released a further evaluation of the DDTC, finding many of the same weaknesses still evident with little clear mitigation, yet suggested it be established on a permanent basis (Department of Justice, Equality and Law Reform, 2010). In the same year, one of the main political parties, Fine Gael, called for drug courts to be 'rolled out nationally' (quoted in Butler, 2013, p. 7). In 2006, the Dublin court was established on a permanent footing and with explicit goals of extending it to all of Dublin. This was despite, over a five-year period, the pilot drug court producing only eleven graduates (Butler, 2013).

Beneath an uneasy political consensus on the viability of the court, qualitative research by Butler highlighted that deep division between the health and criminal justice services persisted. One health worker interviewed described how the seemingly unilateral announcement of the court moving to a permanent basis was an 'own goal' at a time when the court was struggling to show any clear outcomes. In so doing the respondent claimed the courts 'alienated the health service' (quoted in Butler, 2013, p. 7). Meanwhile, a 2007 'Programme for Government' called to 'expand the successful Drug Courts programme' (quoted in Butler, 2013, p. 7).

In 2009, however, in the midst of a national fiscal crisis, the drug court appeared destined for winding down were it not for direct political support for its continuation. The Comptroller and Auditor General called for further research and a comparison with community-based court orders given the low client coverage of the drug court (Butler, 2013). In the same year, the Secretary General of the Department of Justice labelled drug courts a 'well-intentioned experiment which has failed and should now be ended' (quote from paraphrase by Butler, 2013, p. 7). Nevertheless, key politicians rebuked the suggestion and defended the court. Further, the risk of collapse appeared to rally the health and criminal justice sides to overcome their differences (Butler, 2013). Ultimately, the drug court received a reprieve and remained overtly politically popular despite clear misgivings within the civil service.

LATER EVALUATIONS

Civil servants concluded that the drug court was 'solely of symbolic' value and would be continued for that reason, while one of the DDTC health workers described it as 'political /.../ window dressing that suggests you're doing something really radical /.../ and that suits everybody /.../ but it doesn't really address the problem' (Butler, 2013, pp. 11–12). Following the near-death experience, another key *Review of the Drug Treatment Court* by the Department of Justice in 2010 sought to outline ways that the court could increase numbers of participants and argued for a further two years (Department of Justice, Equality and Law Reform, 2010). The report highlighted that from 2001 to 2010, the court had served only 200 clients, with 65% being terminated and 14% graduating. The report made no attempt to determine the follow-on impact on custodial sentences for those terminated from the programme (Butler, 2013). Eight years on from its launch, the DDTC was still facing the same issues as during the initial Farrell Review, albeit on a firmer institutional footing. A more recent 2013 report reiterated many of these issues and demonstrated little clear progress, yet it was not released publicly by the Department of Justice.

Loughran *et al.* point to more recent data showing a total of 602 clients referred to the drug court, with roughly half being found ineligible due to age, location or other mitigating factors (Probation Service, 2013). Of the 294 who were eligible, about two-thirds, or 201, were terminated from the programme, and '[d]espite the expansion to all of Dublin in 2011, referrals and throughput of the [DDTC] still remains low' (Loughran *et al.*, 2015, p. 90).

Butler summarised his qualitative analyses of the experiences of 'professionals and bureaucrats' involved with the operation of the Dublin pilot drug court as follows:

> Those interviewed were generally unconvinced that the American drug court model was technically more effective than more traditional methods of diverting offenders from custodial sentencing into treatment, and tended to see political support for the initiative in terms of the symbolic value of this liberal, humanistic alternative to imprisonment /.../ despite being implemented on a pilot basis in an inner-city area with a well-established high prevalence of problem drug use, the Dublin drug court failed consistently over a 10-year period to attract and retain clients on a scale that would justify maintaining or expanding this scheme /.../ despite such failure, [it] continued to enjoy political support /.../ across all political parties.   (Butler, 2013, pp. 5–6)

Whatever gains were witnessed among some participants, many interviewees were reticent to pin them on the drug court. One Irish judge highlighted 'cherrypicking', something US drug courts have been widely accused of (Sevigny *et al.*, 2013), pointing to the relatively high socioeconomic standing and high social and familial capital of those chosen to showcase the successes of US drug courts (Butler, 2013). As this judge is quoted as saying, 'I've always had a mental reservation about whether this model will work with people who have very poor resources in terms of housing, a stake in society or whatever' (quoted in Butler, 2013, p. 11). Further, respondents viewed diversion into treatment as already well-established and operating independent of the DDTC (Butler, 2013). They further viewed the impulses of politicians as primarily motivated by 'superficial "good news" aspects of the drug courts system', with seemingly little regard for or awareness of the potential impact on 'well-established networks of collaboration between judges, prison systems, Probation Officers and voluntary statutory health and social service systems' (Butler, 2013, p. 12).

THE DRUG COURT GOING FORWARD

The 2009–2016 National Drug Strategy avoided directly engaging with drug courts, instead calling to 'review the current operation and effectiveness of the Drug Court, including the exploration of other international models' (Department of Community, Rural and Gaeltacht Affairs, 2009, p. 98). It highlighted that '[w]hile many agreed with the concept of such a Court, there was little awareness or understanding of the effectiveness of the model. Consequently, there was uncertainty as to whether the model should be expanded, given the level of resources involved' (Department of Community, Rural and Gaeltacht Affairs, 2009, p. 22).

The 2017–2023 National Drug Strategy again sought to avoid direct engagement with the issue, instead deferring to ongoing discussions while suggesting the possibility of an independent review (Department of Health, 2017). Given the outcomes of previous reviews, it is hard to imagine the DDTC showing positive outcomes in terms of value for money or throughput of clients, let alone successful completions. As the recent drug strategy writes,

[t]he Minister for Justice and Equality is examining options as a way forward for the operation of the Drug Treatment Court. The matter will be progressed alongside wider justice reforms that are also under consideration, such as the proposal to establish a Community Court. An independent review of the Drug Treatment Court could inform the Minister's deliberations, and the initiative should continue to be supported in the meantime.

(Department of Health, 2017, p. 56)

Butler's study again provides an important lesson for other jurisdictions embarking on this course. His 2013 study found a general sense that the court would not survive, particularly in periods of fiscal hardship where 'its symbolic value was outweighed by its cost' (Butler, 2013, p. 12). However, one countervailing and arguably prescient view came from a Probation Manager interviewed:

I find it hard to think that it will [survive] in the current context. At the same time, it is one of those things that when it's set up, to terminate it would seem politically like a backward step. Particularly when you have people all over the country trying to set up drug courts.   (Butler, 2013, p. 12)

CONCLUSION

In 1998 the Working Group on a Courts Commission highlighted a United Kingdom Home Office discussion paper on 'Drug treatment and testing orders'. The Home Office report argued that 'the success of any new legislation will depend on the availability of treatment and the resolution of cultural differences between the criminal justice system and treatment providers, underpinned by strong interagency agreements' (quoted in Working Group on a Courts Commission, 1998, p. 27). Butler reinforces this point in the Irish context, highlighting that 'it is superficial and ultimately illusory to see the establishment of drug courts as nothing other than a practical management tool to co-ordinate the working of two sectors;

instead /.../ fundamental cultural differences have arisen' (Butler *et al.*, 2000, p. 56).

Nolan suggests the Irish and Scottish drug court experiments have the most in common: they share a reticence to highlight excessive overseas influence, whether US and/or British; they share general cultural and legal habits; they are imbued with a strong judicial reserve that mitigates against the 'court-as-theatre' dynamic so present in US drug courts; they have been relatively slow in expanding the courts; and they largely reject the TJ ideals that have formed an overt theoretical basis for drug courts in the US, Australia and Canada (Nolan, 2009). Nevertheless, the constitutional and practical problems associated with the DDTC should not be understated. The DDTC, in its current form, appears to create a legal exceptionalism whereby drug-involved clients are not afforded equal protections of due process.

As Butler argued, 'the transfer of the drug court model to Ireland [resulted] from claims that the American drug court model is uniquely effective, both in delivering positive therapeutic outcomes for clients and as a bridge between conflicting philosophical and institutional positions of the healthcare and criminal justice systems' (Butler, 2013). What instead emerges from a close analysis of evaluations and qualitative research is a politically popular failed experiment. Further, aside from direct implementation costs, it bears an unknown opportunity cost in terms of diverting emphasis from reforming broader criminal justice responses to drugs.

Further, the US notion of graduates emerging 'clean' from the drug court process often reflects a tale of redemption within a social milieu where participants deviate from a socially acceptable norm of being law-abiding, 'productive' members of society (Tiger, 2013). As one Irish judge recounts, the 'success' cases he witnessed paraded by US drug court advocates often represented a particular societal subsection with access to familial, educational and social capital. Ultimately, their story appeared one of middle-class 'fall' and 'redemption' (Butler, 2013). This is in direct contrast with the life circumstances of the target Dublin populations, which suffer from generationally entrenched poverty, neglect and exclusion, rendering outcomes such as 'success' and 'abstinence' confused and untethered (Butler, 2013). Such a division between social circumstances adds additional resonance to the question of a Canadian mental health court judge quoted in Nolan: 'Who defines success? What is a therapeutic outcome? By whose standards?' (Nolan, 2009, p. 6).

The Irish case suggests a number of important points. Firstly, one might view US drug courts as a fundamentally US response to a US problem of a rapid growth in incarceration, fuelled by an extreme War on Drugs mentality. Against this generative context, the idea that this has implications for other jurisdictions that never sought to incarcerate their way out of drug problems can seem misguided. Secondly, drug courts and the desire to implement them ultimately represent a lagged reaction by the criminal justice system to a recognition that drug demand issues are far more suitably addressed through complex public health and social service responses. Again, under this reading drug courts can come to be seen not so much as a proactive reform of the criminal justice system, but instead as a reactive effort to adapt to an issue that is increasingly viewed as belonging firmly within the sphere of public health. Drug courts represent a very high-threshold entry point for drug-involved individuals to escape the criminal justice system. They also represent a distraction from the need to integrate very broad low-threshold treatment services into the criminal justice system and ensure adequate diversion is taking place at all points of interaction with law enforcement and the courts. A reliance on judiciary-led 'therapeutic' interventions, while well intentioned, may ultimately prove counterproductive in the better integration of treatment services with drug-involved court clients.

Nolan warns that '[e]mbedded in American problem-solving courts are cultural assumptions that significantly challenge long-held understandings of the meaning and practice of justice – assumptions that when transplanted /.../ may significantly challenge or alter the legal cultures of importing countries' (Nolan, 2009, p. 4). This does not seem to have occurred in a general sense in Ireland but it has resulted in a continued imposition of an external model that never quite fitted the Irish legal or public health systems. Further, it has created a legal exceptionalism for drug-involved offenders that has never been rectified by the Irish legislature and stands, by the admission of drug court judges, in opposition to basic principles of due process. Ultimately, the court appears vulnerable to a High Court challenge.

Two decades after the Working Group convened to examine the drug court model, and more than 15 years since operations proper began, the DDTC has failed to provide a viable model for Ireland. It is not currently conceivable that it can be made to work absent revolutionary changes across relevant institutions, accompanied by a significant increase in funding (at an opportunity cost to more worthwhile treatment interventions).

BIBLIOGRAPHY

Ahern, B. (1997). Introduction by Bertie Ahern, leader of Fianna Fáil. Prudently managing the economy for sustainable growth. Winning the country back for our people. Fianna Fáil 1997 General Election Manifesto. Fianna Fáil, Dublin.

Bean, P. (2002). Drug treatment courts, British style: the drug treatment court movement in Britain. *Substance Use & Misuse* 37, 1595–1614 (https://doi.org/10.1081/JA-120014423).

Butler, S. (2002). The making of the methadone protocol: the Irish system? *Drugs: Education, Prevention and Policy* 9, 311–324 (https://doi.org/10.1080/09687630210148465).

Butler, S. (2013). The symbolic politics of the Dublin drug court: the complexities of policy transfer. *Drugs: Education, Prevention and Policy* 20, 5–13.

Butler, S., Springer, A., and Uhl, A. (2000). A tale of two setors: a critical analysis of the proposal to establish drug courts in the Republic of Ireland. In *Illicit Drugs: Patterns of Use – Patterns of Response*. Studienverlag, Innsbruck.

Csete, J., and Wolfe, D. (2017). Seeing through the public health smokescreen in drug policy. *International Journal of Drug Policy* 43, 91–95 (https://doi.org/10.1016/j.drugpo.2017.02.016).

Daicoff, S. (2000). The role of therapeutic jurisprudence: law as a helping profession. In *Practicing Therapeutic Jurisprudence: Law as a Helping Profession* (edited by Stolle, D. P., Wexler, D. B., and Winick, B. J.). Carolina Academic Press, Durham, NC.

Department of Community, Rural and Gaeltacht Affairs (2009). National drugs strategy (interim), 2009–2016. Department of Community, Rural and Gaeltacht Affairs.

Department of Health (2017). Reducing harm, supporting recovery: a health-led response to drug and alcohol use in Ireland 2017–2025. Department of Health, Dublin.

Department of Health and Human Services (2015). Grants to expand substance abuse treatment capacity in adult and family drug courts. URL: https://www.samhsa.gov/sites/default/files/grants/pdf/ti-15-002-modified-due.pdf (accessed 8 March 2017).

Department of Justice, Equality and Law Reform (2010). Review of the drug treatment court. Department of Justice, Equality and Law Reform, Dublin.

Drug Court Planning Committee (1999). The first report of the Drug Court Planning Committee: pilot project. Report, Stationery Office, Dublin.

Farrell, M. (2002). Final evaluation of the pilot drug court. Courts Service, Dublin.

Fife Drug Court (2002). Fife drug court reference manual.

Franco, C. (2010). Drug courts: background, effectiveness and policy issues for Congress. Congressional Research Service, Washington, DC.

Hot Press Magazine (2018). Philly McMahon, Emmet Kirwan and former Assistant Garda Commissioner, Jack Nolan, among those speaking at Dublin Drug Policy Town Hall meeting. *Hot Press Magazine*, 13 June (https://www.hotpress.com/sex-drugs/philly-mcmahon-emmet-kirwan-and-former-assistant-garda-commissioner-jack-nolan-among-those-speaking-at-dublin-drug-policy-town-hall-meeting-22640244, accessed 15 June 2018).

Hunt, N., and Stevens, A. (2004). Whose harm? Harm reduction and the shift to coercion in UK drug policy. *Social Policy and Society* 3, 333–342 (https://doi.org/10.1017/S1474746404001964).

Jones, E., and Kawalek, A. (2018). Dissolving the stiff upper lip: opportunities and challenges for the mainstreaming of therapeutic jurisprudence in the United Kingdom. *International Journal of Law and Psychiatry*, posted online 8 July (https://doi.org/10.1016/j.ijlp.2018.06.007).

King, M.S. (2008). Restorative justice, therapeutic jurisprudence and the rise of emotionally intelligent justice. *Melbourne University Law Review*, Volume 32.

Loughran, H., and McCann, M. E. (2006). A community drugs study: developing community indicators for problem drug use. National Advisory Committee on Drugs.

Loughran, H., Hohman, M., Carolan, F., and Bloomfield, D. (2015). Practice note: the Irish drug treatment court. *Alcoholism Treatment Quarterly* 33, 82–92 (https://doi.org/10.1080/07347324.2015.982459).

Nolan, J. L. (2009). Legal accents, legal borrowing: the international problem solving court movement. Princeton University Press, Princeton, NJ.

Sevigny, E. L., Fuleihan, B. K., Ferdik, F. V. (2013). Do drug courts reduce the use of incarceration? A meta-analysis. *Journal of Criminal Justice* 41, 416–425 (http://dx.doi.org/10.1016/j.jcrimjus.2013.06.005).

Stolle, D. P., Wexler, D. B., and Winick, B. J. (2000). *Practicing Therapeutic Jurisprudence: Law as a Helping Profession*. Carolina Academic Press, Durham, NC.

Teubner, G. (2001). Legal irritants: how unifying law ends up in new divergences. In *Varieties of Capitalism: The Institutional Foundations of Comparative Advantage* (edited by Hall, P. A., and Soskice, D.). Oxford University Press.

Tiger, R. (2013). *Judging Addicts: Drug Courts and Coercion in the Justice System (Alternative Criminology)*. NYU Press.

US Government Accountability Office (2011). Adult drug courts: studies show courts reduce recidivism, but DOJ could enhance future performance measure revision efforts (No. GAO-12-53). GAO, Washington, DC.

Working Group on a Courts Commission (1998). Drug Courts (No. 5). Dublin.

CHAPTER 4

Drug Policy, Therapeutic Jurisprudence and Criminal Justice in Brazil

By Luiz Guilherme Mendes de Paiva[1]

The relationship between drug policy and criminal justice in Brazil is intimate and problematic. Despite a well-intentioned legal framework, supposedly aimed at diverting drug users from the criminal justice system, low-level drug dealers and highly vulnerable people, many of whom are problematic drug users who occasionally commit small property crimes or are caught in the grey zone between drug consumption and micro-trafficking, fill the proverbially overcrowded Brazilian prison system.

This chapter aims to provide an overview of the legal framework and judicial activity on the matter, and critically evaluate the development of alternatives to address the rising drug-related incarceration rates. It analyses judicial behaviour towards drug offences and its deep roots in Brazilian inequality, and explores the vulnerability profile of people arrested for drug-related crimes, for whom the criminal justice system is completely unprepared to provide meaningful support. It also analyses the local drug court experience – the so-called Therapeutic Jurisprudence programme – pointing out the reasons for their lack of sustainability and eventual near-disappearance. The chapter concludes with an assessment of a promising local experience to enhance cooperation between criminal courts and social and health services.

1   Thanks to F. Policarpo and M. A. B. Weigert for their research contributions, and to J. O. Carlos for feedback provided on the first draft of this chapter. Special thanks to H. Rodrigues, coordinator of the Network Project in São Paulo, for generously contributing the results of that pilot project.

BACKGROUND

Brazil holds an unflattering third place in the ranking of countries with the largest prison populations in the world. There are currently more than 720,000 people in state and federal prisons, an increase of 300% in 20 years. Official data shows the national prison occupancy level at 198%, peaking at almost 500% in the northern state of Amazonas (Departamento Penitenciário Nacional, 2016). Nationally, with a total population of 208 million, the incarceration rate is currently at 352 per 100,000 people, and rising. Pre-trial arrests account for more than 40% of the prison population.

In 2014, drug offences surpassed theft as the most frequent cause of arrest in the country. Before the 2006 Drug Law was passed, the proportion of people incarcerated for drug offences was around 10%; in 2016, 26% of men and 62% of women within the prison system were accused of, or sentenced for, drug law violations.

This significant incarceration effect resulted in many ways from the promulgation of the so-called New Drug Law of 2006. This law promised a more rational and proportional legal framework for drug offences. Legislators stated that the drug problem would no longer be solely a matter for criminal law: state and society must share responsibility for prevention, treatment and social reintegration of drug (dependent) users, based on respect for their fundamental rights, 'especially regarding their autonomy and their freedom'.[2]

Brazilian drug legislation has always been essentially repressive in character. The 2006 law replaced a 1976 law, the articles of which held an exceptionally punitive bias. Indeed, the latter was conceived during the military dictatorship, symbolising a time when the drug problem was simply taken as a matter for law enforcement.

For that reason, the new legislation was hailed as a breakthrough in recognising the drug problem as multifaceted, demanding broader and more diverse policies than mere repression. In a controversial move at the time, the new law 'depenalised' possession of drugs for

---

2   Law 11,343, Article 4.I: 'The Principles of the National Drug Policy System'.

personal use, meaning that, while still a crime, it should no longer lead to incarceration.[3]

In spite of the symbolic advances, however, repression remained as the key dynamic. To compensate for the 'depenalization' of drug possession for personal use, the new law severely increased punishment for drug trafficking without adequately differentiating between them. There is no quantity threshold explicitly distinguishing between drug possession and drug trafficking offences, and in practice the decision of which offence an individual is charged with rests solely with the police. The result is predictable: people who use drugs and micro-traffickers, and especially those caught between these roles, are consistently arrested and face severely disproportionate prison sentences for drug trafficking, regardless of their lack of individual relevance to, or agency over, the functioning of the local drug market.

Since the new law came into force, several investigations have sought to identify and disaggregate the profiles of arrestees, seizures and persons incarcerated for drug offences. In 2009, researchers from Brasília and Rio de Janeiro noted that 80% of people arrested for drug offences during the previous year were caught alone, unarmed and with small amounts of drugs (Boiteux *et al.*, 2009). These findings were reinforced by a 2011 study that analysed police reports on drug trafficking in São Paulo: more than 80% of arrests were made by military police on regular patrols, not preceded by any investigation. Average seizure size amounted to 66.5 grams. Three-quarters of those arrested were between 18 and 29 years of age, and 57% had no previous criminal record. Nine out of ten remained in pre-trial custody (Marques *et al.*, 2011).

These trends persisted in the following years. Despite rulings from the Supreme Court and a new criminal procedure law aimed at persuading judges to adopt alternatives to pre-trial arrests, police activity remained the same. In 2015, a new report indicated that

---

3   Possession of illegal drugs for personal use remains a crime, and a conviction leads to a criminal record, which can prevent access to non-custodial measures in the future.

the majority of people arrested for drug offences in São Paulo were non-white, young and with low education levels (Carlos, 2015). It also showed that, in most cases, the quantities of drugs seized in the arrests were very small. The irrelevance of most arrests for drug offences in terms of drug seizures is strongly demonstrated by a report on drug-related arrests in Rio de Janeiro between 2010 and 2016 (Instituto de Segurança Pública do Rio de Janeiro, 2016): 98% of arrests amounted to 14% of total marijuana seizures in the period. In 50% of arrest cases for marijuana, 10 grammes or less were seized. The data for cocaine are equally stark: only 1% of total seizures captured more than two kilogrammes (see Figure 1).

The most recent data on how the judiciary reacts to this massive influx of small drug offences was outlined by a 2018 report from the State Public Defence Office in Rio de Janeiro. Analysing thousands of judicial convictions for drug trafficking and 'conspiracy to commit drug trafficking', it confirmed previous findings on police proceedings, the profile of people arrested and the small amounts of drugs seized. It also shed light on how the judiciary relies on police reports as the only evidence in most conviction cases (Haber *et al.*, 2018).

All this information provides a clear picture of how the police and criminal justice systems work with regard to drug offences. Large numbers of non-violent drug offenders are being arrested and detained for ever-longer periods in a vastly overcrowded prison system, mostly due to the possession of relatively small amounts of illicit drugs. These offenders share a well-defined racial and social vulnerability profile: a reflection of the endemic racism and inequality in Brazilian society. It is not surprising that the same profile is also shared by the vast majority of people murdered in the country and by those living in open-air drug markets in many Brazilian cities (Fundação Oswaldo Cruz, 2014; Cerqueira *et al.*, 2017).

The focus on small retail drug offences is not only ineffective, but also vastly counterproductive. Brazilian prisons are effectively run by prison gangs, whose influence is felt way beyond penitentiary walls (Dias, 2017). Today, highly sophisticated criminal organisations control most drug trafficking routes within the country and manage several illegal activities in the streets of cities like São Paulo (Feltran, 2012). By incarcerating thousands of low-level, non-violent drug offenders, the criminal justice system acts like a state-sponsored recruiting system for violent organised crime (Lessing, 2017).

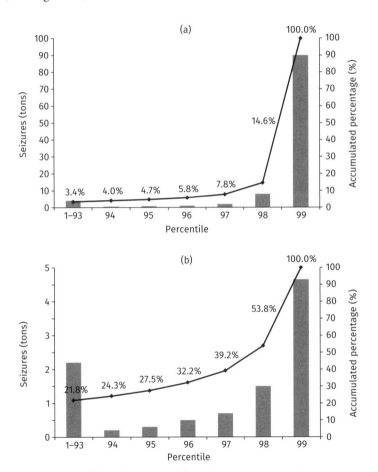

Figure 1. Mass of (a) marijuana and (b) cocaine seizures, by police reports and accumulated seizures, in Rio de Janeiro from 2010 to 2015. (*Source*: adapted from Instituto de Segurança Pública do Rio de Janeiro (2016, pp. 13–14).)

CRIMINAL JUSTICE AND SOCIAL VULNERABILITY

There is a striking resemblance between the profiles of incarcerated and homeless people, particularly those living in the surroundings of open crack-cocaine scenes in major Brazilian cities. These groups share vulnerability factors such as race (non-whites), low education level, being of a young age and having no routine work or stable housing (Toledo *et al.*, 2017), and they have a disproportionately high prevalence of problematic drug use. The life trajectory of this population frequently involves rotating between prison, homelessness and drug use (Mallart and Rui, 2017). There is also a very low access to health and social services, which reinforces their exclusion and vulnerability (Dias *et al.*, 2011).[4]

It is worth noting that, in cities like São Paulo and Rio de Janeiro, social and health services are available for the most vulnerable population, such as users in open drug scenes. Despite the limitations of an underfunded public health system and the tense coexistence of harm-reduction programmes and abstinence-based drug treatment services (public and private, including religious therapeutic communities), past city administrations have sought to provide housing, social and health care focused at reducing the visible and highly unpopular 'cracklands' in city centres. However, these initiatives have proven unable to reach any significant numbers of drug users and link them with municipal networks of regular services.

In this scenario, the criminal justice system is frequently the only public service that consistently reaches these vulnerable groups. Detention rates among crack users in open drug scenes are much higher than in the general population, mostly, but not exclusively, for drug-related offences (Fundação Oswaldo Cruz, 2014, p. 65). This adds to a widespread scepticism among judges and public prosecutors regarding alternatives to incarceration, which leaves two options on the table after an arrest: releasing a defendant or imposing pre-trial

---

4   It should be pointed out that mortality rates among crack-cocaine users are much higher than in the general population, homicide being the major cause of death.

detention. The fact that judges often identify a greater risk of recidivism in vulnerability factors such as drug addiction and homelessness, combined with the lack of options within the criminal justice system to address these factors, partially explains the staggering rates of pre-trial detention in Brazil, reaching 40% in 2016 (Departamento Penitenciário Nacional, 2016, p. 13). Attending a custody hearing in Sao Paulo in 2015, this author witnessed a reluctant judge impose a pre-trial arrest for a female defendant accused of a minor larceny after being informed that she had already been arrested and released the month before for the same reason. The judge noted that the accused was obviously in need of rehabilitation or even basic social services but stated that providing them was beyond his reach: 'I know that prison won't do her much good, but what can I do? If I let her go, she will be back in here in no time.'

DRUG COURTS IN BRAZIL

In this scenario, one could honestly believe that drug treatment courts could be an efficient alternative to provide assistance for people who would otherwise go to prison. The implementation of drug courts was one of the pillars of the Organization of American States 2010 hemispheric strategy, but diplomatic efforts around its adoption in Brazil began earlier. The 2002 US International Narcotics Control Strategy Report states that in the previous year,

> the USG financed and organized drug court conferences in Brazil, providing U.S. speakers, as well as trips to the U.S. by GOB [Government of Brazil] state justice officials to observe first-hand how drug courts operate in the U.S.
>
> (US Department of State, 2002, p. 11).

Indeed, a specific drug court model was trialled in several Brazilian jurisdictions in the early 2000s. Usually called therapeutic jurisprudence, these initiatives presented themselves as an alternative to regular criminal procedures for problematic drug users, 'prioritizing offender recovery and reparation to the victims' (Achutti, 2006, p. 66). The term therapeutic jurisprudence was deliberately adopted to differentiate itself from the US Drug Court model, presenting the programme as a genuinely local conception and facilitating its acceptance by the justice system, even though most judges and prosecutors pioneering the local initiatives were involved in the cooperation efforts of the US State Department. As stated by the former president of the now-defunct National Therapeutic Jurisprudence Association, Ricardo de Oliveira Silva:

> the Therapeutic Jurisprudence concept enshrines the highest principles of law in the relation between the State and the citizen, in the search for a solution not only to the conflict with the law, but also to the social problems of individuals and the community and health problems related to drug use /.../ [It is] a genuinely Brazilian denomination and clearly defining its purposes.
>
> (Lima, 2009, p. 131 [free translation])

A national organisation of judges and prosecutors was created to develop a countrywide movement of Therapeutic Jurisprudence Programs, with strong links to the International Association of Drug Courts Professionals and political support from the federal government, declaring the need to raise awareness of the cause (Weigert, 2010).

One of the first pilots was assembled in 2001 in Rio de Janeiro, creating specific diversion mechanisms for young persons involved in drug offences or who committed criminal violations under the influence of drugs. If an alternative to incarceration was available, the defendant was offered rehabilitation treatment, in connection with local health services. The judges could also impose compulsory attendance in prevention programmes or treatment: failure to comply would reopen the criminal procedure (Weigert, 2010, p. 137).

The experience in Rio illustrates the several limitations of the therapeutic jurisprudence model in Brazil. These limitations are related to its scope, its lack of proper incentives, its failure to understand the wider social and health care needs of target groups, and institutional obstacles, all of which prevented this drug court model from gaining national scale and eventually led to their slow termination.

(a) Scope. The therapeutic jurisprudence (TJ) model of drug courts in Brazil was not implemented by a federal law, so it naturally had to adapt to the established laws and legal procedures. This meant that most experiences were limited either to the juvenile system or to adults accused of drug possession, a low-level criminal offence that would not lead to prison sentences in the first place, even before the 2006 Law. In other words, it was not conceived to reach people who would otherwise be incarcerated, but to provide better treatment to a target group who would be subject to a non-custodial measure.

In Brazilian law, adults accused of low-level crimes (offences with a maximum prison sentence of two years or less) are submitted to the Special Criminal Court system, with simplified proceedings and pre- and post-conviction diversion measures. The TJ programme in Rio de Janeiro was assembled as one of the many post-adjudication services available to persons accused of drug possession, ostensibly as a means to provide assistance to 'drug users' (Policarpo, 2015, p. 147).

It was an expansion of a similar programme created a few months earlier, within the Rio de Janeiro Juvenile Court, which took advantage of legislation allowing the substitution of custodial measures for health and psychological treatment for underage drug offenders (Lage *et al.*, 2012). The explicit goal of both programmes was to promote 'effective mechanisms for rehabilitation' of drug users, considering that establishing such mechanisms required cooperation between several public services and institutions.[5]

---

5   The Therapeutic Jurisprudence Program within the juvenile court system was created in 2001 by a State Court act (Provimento 20/2001), and expanded in 2002 to the Special Criminal Court (Ato Executivo Conjunto 41/2002). The latter act stated, 'prison sentences /.../ alone do not fulfil the public need for prevention of criminal acts associated to use and addiction of narcotic substances'. Still, the new system was limited to low-level crimes for which no custodial penalties would be imposed.

The same scope limitation is found in the first documented TJ programme in the country, initiated in 1999 in the southern state of Rio
Grande do Sul. It was directed at low-level offenders who were also
considered as persons with drug addiction. It intended to provide

> treatment for drug addiction, which will give the offender/patient
> the skills and abilities to stabilize its illness, acquiring better quality
> of life, and even stop offending behaviour.
>
> (Silva and Freitas, 2008, p. 1)

The Rio Grande do Sul programme had a larger scope than its
Rio de Janeiro counterpart, as it was also available for some domestic violence cases. A similar programme installed in a local court in
2002, in the city of São Paulo, also encompassed traffic offences and
other non-violent misdemeanours (Lamarck, 2015). However, all
major experiences in the country were limited to low-level offences,
for which no custodial penalty would be imposed.

Even non-judicial programmes such as the Therapeutic Jurisprudence Centre, created in 2001 at the State Court of the north-eastern
state of Pernambuco to connect local jurisdictions to different services related to drug policy, limited themselves to 'offenders related
to psychoactive substances' who committed low-level crimes (Lima,
2009, p. 158).

By analysing the programmes, their scope and their declared
objectives, it becomes clear that drug courts – as implemented in
Brazil – could not possibly present themselves as alternatives to
incarceration, as their target groups would not be subject to custodial
sentences. Therefore, it failed to address the most striking problem
in the Brazilian criminal justice system, which is over-incarceration
related to drug offences.

While it is fair to say that a major widening of the scope of drug
courts would demand implausible legal reform, it should be mentioned that some improvements could be designed within the current
legal framework. For example, simple larceny and micro-trafficking
are still offences that frequently lead to incarceration, but in such
cases judges are allowed to impose alternatives to incarceration.

Unfortunately, none of the analysed programmes were available for these crimes.

(b) Lack of incentives. The fact that TJ programmes in Brazil were limited to offences that would not lead to custodial sentences also led to a profound lack of incentives both for offenders, who must comply with the additional burden of the TJ system, and for the bureaucratic bodies within the court system itself, who have simpler, cheaper non-custodial measures available to offer.

From the offender's legal perspective, the Brazilian model lacked the basic operational incentive of drug court systems, which is complying with a treatment programme in exchange for the deferment or suspension of a prison sentence. There is little to promote obedience in relation to the programme conditions. Even when the diversion programmes effectively provided new or facilitated paths to treatment services, failure to comply would cause – in the worst-case scenario – the offender to return to the regular criminal procedure, where he or she would likely receive a milder sentence than treatment itself (Lima, 2009; Lage *et al.*, 2012).

This is even more striking when one observes that the treatment options available for offenders in the TJ programmes are the same insufficient services provided to every citizen: outpatient public health services, in-patient clinics or private, religious therapeutic communities, or therapy within abstinence-based groups such as Alcoholics Anonymous (AA) or Narcotics Anonymous (NA). It is worth mentioning that drug testing was not a central feature in most programmes: a major difference between Brazilian and US drug court models. While some authors say it reflects an intentional separation between health and justice, characteristic of the TJ movement in Brazil, reports have mentioned that urine testing was performed in the early stages of some programmes but was discontinued due to a lack of adequate testing material (Lage *et al.*, 2012, p. 387).[6]

---

6   The authors mentioned that urine tests in some Rio de Janeiro courts were only performed for the duration of resources donated by the US Embassy (p. 380).

In fact, Brazilian TJ courts could not rely on the US Drug Treatment Court model of providing treatment that was otherwise unavailable to the public as a judicial bargain, for several reasons. Firstly, it is questionable under Brazilian law whether a specific public drug-treatment programme could be devised for criminal offenders without violating the principles of the Unified Health Service, SUS (the national public health care system). Secondly, under the same principles, it is even more questionable whether the judicial system could deny treatment to a drug-dependent offender who refused to adhere to the drug court regulations. These were the most important factors in the reluctance of the Brazilian government to officially embrace the drug court initiatives within OAS-CICAD.[7]

A further important limitation is the major restriction on bargaining within the prosecutorial and judicial system. Unlike most common law jurisdictions, Brazilian prosecutors are not allowed to refrain from pursuing conviction for a crime that comes to their knowledge. With no prosecutorial discretion, alternatives to incarceration can only be offered within the strict limits of the existing legal framework, which partially explains the limited scope of TJ programmes in the country.

Procedural efficacy was also a major obstacle in scaling up the programmes within the criminal justice system. Analysing the Rio de Janeiro TJ programme, Policarpo (2015) concluded that judges and court assistants were effectively avoiding referring offenders to the TJ programme because those cases would take longer to be closed compared with the simpler, faster imposition of ordinary non-custodial measures such as fines or community services. Further complicating the matter, the Special Criminal Court established its own link with public health services, NA and AA. The initial goal of TJ – to offer an adequate judicial service to drug users – became subordinated to procedural celerity, for which the regular court system in Rio de Janeiro engaged in a 'bureaucratic boycott' of the TJ programme.

---

7   The Inter-American Drug Abuse Control Commission (CICAD) within the Oganisation of American States (OAS).

(c) Insufficient approach. The TJ model adopted in Brazil departed from the assumption that drug use, or drug dependence, was the preponderant factor for a significant number of criminal offences in the country. The Rio de Janeiro 2002 Act goes as far as stating that 'an expressive number of crimes committed in this State [are] related to illegal substance use, a fact also noticed by news outlets'. This assumption often relates to a wider perception within Brazilian society that drug use is responsible for many social problems, such as violence, homelessness and a sense of moral degradation – which runs beyond class distinctions.

There is little evidence, however, that drug use is the main driver of criminal offences. In fact, it is hardly tenable that drug use is the main social problem. Available data unequivocally show that regular and problematic drug users, especially those with patterns of open-air drug use, are people with a personal trajectory of social exclusion and vulnerability, in which drug use is only part of the problem (Rui, 2014; Rui *et al.*, 2016; Souza, 2016).

Besides, as demonstrated in the introduction of this paper, people within the regular criminal justice system represent the most vulnerable strata of Brazilian society, for whom a myriad of (often unavailable) social, psychological, health, housing and other basic public services are essential.

Even if they were efficient in providing adequate health services to their 'clients', drug courts – and the TJ model in particular – failed to present themselves as a meaningful tool to address the cycle of crime and exclusion that fuels recidivism, by limiting themselves to focusing on drug use as the main individual problem of people captured by the criminal justice system.

One of the key TJ strategies set by the OAS-CICAD Drug Treatment Courts handbook states that the judge should ask participants to

> formulate rehabilitation plans setting out their goals for their time in the program and beyond, and the strategies they intend to pursue in order to achieve these goals.   (Wexler and King, 2013, p. 38)

While this could be a useful strategy in cases involving individuals with any kind of social support, it may feel almost whimsical to those who have lost most of their formal and informal social connections and for whom making plans for the future is not an option.

Investigating crack-cocaine users in Brazil, Arenari and Dutra (2016) refer to local studies on the personal trajectory of problematic drug users, typically involving disintegration of relations of reciprocity and affection in the family sphere, dropping out of school and precarious insertion in the labor market. The authors coined a sociological term, which could be roughly translated as 'hypertrophy of the present', to describe a condition where life is a succession of unrelated 'presents', where no future can even be devised (Arenari and Dutra, 2016, p. 193). Unfortunately, this is also the case for a majority of offenders who routinely orbit the Brazilian justice system.

A proper TJ programme, relevant to this group, should encompass a series of social objectives to make possible a rehabilitation plan to allow these individuals to establish their personal goals and organise their futures, even if only in the short term. By failing to comprehend drug use in the larger picture of social vulnerability, TJ programmes in Brazil were totally incapable of achieving this outcome.

As in most Latin American drug court experiences, TJ initiatives in Brazil lack detailed information about participants, metrics and evaluations. A partial exception is the Rio de Janeiro Therapeutic Jurisprudence Program, which was submitted to an external evaluation in 2004 that highlighted its low capacity to provide assistance to a significant number of offenders. Commenting on the fact that, in three years, only 33 people were referred to the TJ programme by the court of Niterói, the second most populous city in the state of Rio de Janeiro, one social worker said:

> we lack infrastructure /…/ It is better [the judge] send fewer people, and do a good job in the little we can.   (Lage *et al.*, 2012, p. 385)

COURTS AND WELFARE: ALTERNATIVES

These limitations and contradictions could offer a possible explanation for the low practical and political impact produced by TJ experiences within the Brazilian justice system. From several promising initiatives in different parts of the country, few drug courts remain in place, and the ones that do are often dependent on the personal will of judges and prosecutors.

It would be unwise, however, to state that courts have no possible role within drug policy apart from applying custodial and non-custodial penalties to offenders, with or without drug-related problems. In fact, considering that persons captured by the criminal justice system are socially vulnerable and often very hard to reach through regular social and health services, their contact with the court may provide an important opportunity for their inclusion in the existing network of social, health, housing and other public services.

Besides, a carefully designed, court-supervised program linking the criminal justice system to existing services could also address the already-mentioned complaints of judges and prosecutors, who may be willing to consider non-custodial measures if they feel that highly vulnerable offenders will be looked after by other public services. A pilot programme that took place in 2016 and 2017 in São Paulo could provide an indication of how courts can be a useful tool to address this complex situation. It showed promising results in connecting different aspects of the criminal justice system and the wider public services network in a cheaper, simpler and more consequential manner than the traditional models.

NETWORK PROJECT – CUSTODY HEARING UNIT (SÃO PAULO)

While São Paulo accounts for 20% of the Brazilian population, it accounts for 40% of the people incarcerated in the country. In the state capital, hundreds of people are arrested every day, the vast majority by the military police *in flagrante delicto,* i.e. without previous investigation. Until 2015, most would remain in prison until the first hearing by the judge of the case, which could take months. However, an administrative reform in São Paulo Court ensured that every person arrested must be presented to a judge within 24 hours to verify the legality of the arrest.

The custody hearings, now a countrywide practice, are an effort to reduce the unacceptable pre-trial detention rates. They also present an opportunity to use hearings not only as a procedural step, but to connect the existing social, health, housing and other services to a highly vulnerable, hard-to-reach population.

In general, judges and prosecutors lack confidence in alternatives to incarceration. They do not trust the effectiveness and impact of non-custodial measures, and feel there are only two real options before them: either release the offender or arrest them. Research has shown that drug addiction, homelessness and even the place of residence – if one lives in regions supposedly dominated by gangs – often serve as aggravating factors, rather than mitigating circumstances, since judges identify greater risk of recidivism and do not recognise existing alternatives to incarceration as adequate solutions to the problem. Under these circumstances, a successful project should present itself as an assurance that a non-custodial decision could trigger positive outcomes.

In the São Paulo Central Criminal Court, where an average of 180 people arrested within the previous 24 hours are presented to a judge from the custody-hearing unit every day, a pilot project was assembled with federal funding and using existing structures from the state administration. A team of six social workers, psychologists and legal practitioners were available to review the personal conditions of offenders for whom a pre-trial release was granted and who declared having problems associated with drug use, regardless of the criminal accusation.[8] The Oswaldo Cruz Foundation, a public research centre from the Ministry of Health, coordinated the project.

---

8   According to Brazilian law, it is not possible to arrest *in flagrante delicto* for a low-level offence (sentences up to two years). So the project, by design, was directed towards offenders who could receive a prison sentence at the end of the judicial proceeding.

The project had three objectives. The first was addressing the specific needs of these people and connecting them to existing services according to their specificities and availability. This could be labour intensive, because most offenders were so vulnerable that they were in no condition to find the address of the health centre, or even to present proper documentation to enrol in a welfare programme. Sometimes, the public services themselves were not prepared to deal with this population, making it essential that the social workers were present.

The second objective was to expand and prepare the existing welfare network, however precarious, to absorb the new demand. The project coordinators were responsible for contacting health, social, housing and other public services at city, state and federal levels to open new paths and find new opportunities that could be made available to the target group.

The third, and most indirect, objective was to convince judges from the custody-hearing unit that referring an offender to the project was a good alternative to a pre-trial detention. Reports were regularly presented to the coordinator judge, and workshops and seminars were organised to raise awareness, discuss the results and possible improvements. The expectation was to lower the pre-trial detention rates, especially in drug-related cases.

The project was executed from May 2016 to November 2017. During this time, judges referred 192 people to the service. Seventeen were arrested again, 46 were not monitored (death, refusal or inability to locate) and 135 remained under regular monitoring. The social profile of this group confirms the diagnosis of previous research: 80% were men, 51% had incomplete elementary education, and 54% had precarious housing or were homeless. All of them, as a condition of referral, reported health problems related to drug use, and 44% reported using multiple drugs – the vast majority mentioned using alcohol and crack-cocaine.

During the interviews, beneficiaries showed little understanding of the legal procedure in which they had just been involved, and they wanted to leave the courtroom as soon as possible. The high-vulnerability profile was manifested in the provision of basic needs such as showers, clean clothing, personal hygiene items and, mostly, access to shelters. Healthcare needs were not limited to drug use or mental health issues, but also for dental care, HIV testing and care, skin wounds and other related basic and urgent demands.

It cannot be overstated that there are proper public services available in the city of São Paulo to address these basic needs. However, the target group has a strong disadvantage in accessing public welfare programmes and institutions. The project allowed the unfortunate and traumatic experience of contact with the justice system to serve as a tool for establishing more relevant and adequate health, social and housing services for this population.

At the institutional level, the project was successful in establishing formal and informal cooperation with public mental healthcare centres, public shelters, documentation centres and other services. However, these links were too reliant on personal networks established between social workers, a problem also identified in reports of several TJ initiatives. The next step would be to consolidate this connection between these services and the courtroom clientele.

During the functioning of the pilot project, pre-trial detentions reduced from 61% to 50% in São Paulo Criminal Court. However, due to the relatively small number of people referred by the judges, it is not possible to attribute this reduction to the project. It is more likely a conjunction of factors, attributed to the dynamics of the custody hearing itself and the accumulated experience of judges in addressing never-ending waves of low-level cases that would eventually lead to non-custodial sentences. It would demand further investigation to identify if workshops and project reports played their part in increasing the odds of judges deciding for pre-trial release in ordinary cases, and whether involvement in the programme would be taken into account during the trial.

Despite its short duration and small scale, it was successful in demonstrating the possibility of using existing structures to access a vulnerable population, frequently accessed only by security and criminal justice structures. It also differed from Brazilian TJ models by not limiting itself to low-level offenders, and for effectively seeking to serve as a substitute for custodial measures. The total budget was limited to small-scale operational costs (transportation, stationery, etc.) and the team's salaries, making it a very cost-effective alternative. Unfortunately, changes in the administration at the federal and state court levels resulted in the termination of the programme by the end of the pilot.[9]

CONCLUSION

Drug courts programmes in Brazil were inspired by the US model, but local particularities prevented their implementation according to the key components of that system. Legal and institutional restrictions and, particularly, a focus on low-level offences that would not lead to custodial sentences led to limited, local initiatives that did not gain national relevance.

Even if the Brazilian programmes were able to implement drug courts as intended by its proponents, it would likely be unsuccessful in pursuing its goal of promoting 'effective mechanisms for rehabilitation' of drug users. The many problems inherent to the model – extensively debated in recent reports such as 'Drug courts: equivocal evidence on a popular intervention' from Open Society Foundations (Csete and Tomasini-Joshi, 2015) and 'Drug courts in the Americas' from the Social Science Research Council (2018) – adds to the complex pattern of exclusion, racism and violence victimising Brazil's most vulnerable population. Any approach that highlights drug use as the main driver of recurrent criminal behaviour, and presents the criminal justice system as a means to address it, seems to run directly counter to the best evidence we have.

This does not mean that courts should not have any significant role in improving services for people with drug-use problems. Brazil

---

9   In September 2018, a city healthcare team was assigned to the Central Criminal Court, offering treatment to defendants who are released at custodial hearings. Its design is similar to the previous Network Project, and preliminary results are yet to be announced.

is in the unfortunate position of having the criminal justice system as the most efficient public service to reach certain vulnerable populations. Offering relevant public services such as social, health and housing to this specific group will be useful both to address the specific needs of the individuals and to try to reverse the over-incarceration pattern related to drug-related offences.

However, these efforts must not obscure the fact that criminal justice is ineffective and often counterproductive in addressing complex social problems. It is clear that drug use should not be a criminal issue and there is an urgent need to address rampant over-incarceration that is in many ways a direct result of aggressive prosecution of the War on Drugs. Priority should be given to preventing the unnecessary imprisonment of people with drug-related problems, whether or not it is for drug-related crimes.

REFERENCES

Achutti, D. (2006). A crise do processo penal na sociedade contemporânea: uma análise a partir das novas formas de administração da justiça criminal. Catholic University of Rio Grande do Sul.

Arenari, B., and Dutra, R. (2016). A construção social da condição de pessoa: premissas para romper o círculo vicioso de exclusão e uso problemático de crack. In *Crack e Exclusão Social* (edited by Souza, J.), pp. 191–222. Ministério da Justiça e Cidadania, Brasília.

Boiteux, L., Castilho, E. W. V, Vargas, B., Batista, V. O., Prado, G. L. M., and Japiassu, C. E. A. (2009). Drug trafficking and constitution. Brasília. Available at http://pensando.mj.gov.br/wp-content/uploads/2015/07/01Pensando_Direito3.pdf.

Carlos, J. O. (2015). Drug policy and incarceration in Brazil. Available at http://idpc.net/publications/2015/06/idpc-briefing-paper-drug-policy-in-brazil-2015.

Cerqueira, D., Sergio de Lima, R., Bueno, S., Valencia, L. I., Hanashiro, O., Machado, P. H., and dos Santos Lima, A. (2017). Atlas da Violência. Rio de Janeiro. Available at http://www.ipea.gov.br/atlasviolencia/download/2/atlas-2017.

Csete, J., and Tomasini-Joshi, D. (2015). Drug courts: equivocal evidence on a popular intervention. New York. Available at https://www.open societyfoundations.org/reports/drug-courts-equivocal-evidence-popul ar-intervention.

Departamento Penitenciário Nacional (2016). Levantamento Nacional de Informações Penitenciárias – Junho de 2016. Brasília. Available at http://www.justica.gov.br/news/ha-726-712-pessoas-presas-no-brasil/ relatorio_2016_junho.pdf.

Dias, A. C., Araujo, M. R., Sesso, R. C., Laranjeira, R., Dunn, J., and Castro, V. D. (2011). Mortality rate among crack/cocaine-dependent patients: a 12-year prospective cohort study conducted in Brazil. *Journal of Substance Abuse Treatment* 41(3), 273–278.

Dias, C. N. (2017). Encarceramento, seletividade e opressão: a 'crise carcerária' como projeto político. Caderno Análise, No. 28/2017. Available at http://library.fes.de/pdf-files/bueros/brasilien/13444.pdf.

Feltran, G. S. (2012). Governo que produz crime, crime que produz governo: o dispositivo de gestão do homicídio em São Paulo (1992–2012). *Revista Brasileira de Segurança Pública* 6(2).

Fundação Oswaldo Cruz (2014). Pesquisa nacional sobre o uso de crack - Quem são os usuários de crack e/ou similares do Brasil? Quantos são nas capitais brasileiras? Rio de Janeiro. Available at https://www.arca. fiocruz.br/bitstream/icict/10019/2/UsoDeCrack.pdf.

Haber, C., Maciel, N. C. A., and Pinto Junior, J. A. (2018). Tráfico e sentenças judiciais: uma análise das justificativas na aplicação da lei de drogas no RJ. Rio de Janeiro. Available at https://www.conjur.com.br/ dl/palavra-policiais-foi-unica-prova-54.pdf.

Instituto de Segurança Pública do Rio de Janeiro (2016). Panorama das Apreensões de Drogas no Rio de Janeiro – 2010–2016. Available at http://arquivos.proderj.rj.gov.br/isp_imagens/uploads/RelatorioDrog as2016.pdf.

Lage, L., Lima, L. L., and Souza da Silva, S. (2012). O Programa de Justiça Terapêutica do Estado do Rio de Janeiro. *Revista Estudos de Sociologia* 17(33), 375–398.

Lamarck, S. (2015). Análise do Programa Justiça Terapêutica no município de Goiânia nos anos de 2010–2013. Catholic University of Goiania.

Lessing, B. (2017). Counterproductive punishment: how prison gangs undermine state authority. *Rationality and Society* 29(3), 257–297 (doi: 10.1177/1043463117701132).

Lima, F. A. (2009). Justiça Terapêutica: em busca de um novo paradigma. University of São Paulo.

Mallart, F., and Rui, T. (2017). Cadeia ping-pong: entre o dentro e o fora das muralhas. *Ponto Urbe*, 21. Available at http://journals.openedition. org/pontourbe/3620.

Marques, G., Oi, A. H., Rocha, T. T., and Lagatta, P. (2011). Pre-trial arrests and Drug Law. University of São Paulo. Available at http:// www.nevusp.org/downloads/down254.pdf.

Policarpo, F. (2015). Da Justiça Terapêutica à atual Lei de Drogas: o modo como o sistema de justiça criminal lida com os consumidores de drogas. *O Público e o Privado* 26(2), 139–158.

Rui, T. (2014). Nas tramas do crack: etnografia da abjeção. São Paulo.

Rui, T., Fiore, M., and Tófoli, L. F. (2016). Pesquisa preliminar de avaliação do programa 'De Braços Abertos'. São Paulo. Available at http:// pbpd.org.br/wp-content/uploads/2016/12/Pesquisa-De-Braços-Abertos-1-2.pdf.

Silva, R., and Freitas, C. (2008). Justiça Terapêutica: um programa judicial de redução do dano social. Available at http://www.premioinnovare. com.br/praticas/l/justica-terapeutica-um-programa-judicial-de-reducao-do-dano-social-2127.

Social Science Research Council (2018). Drug courts in the Americas. Social Science Research Council, New York. Available at https://www .ssrc.org/publications/view/drug-courts-in-the-americas/.

Souza, J. (2016). Crack e Exclusão Social. Brasília. Available at http://ittc .org.br/wp-content/uploads/2016/07/Livro_Crack_e_exclusão_social _Digital_WEB.pdf.

Toledo, L., Cano, I., Bastos, L., Bertoni, N., and Bastos, F. I. (2017). Criminal justice involvement of crack cocaine users in the city of Rio de Janeiro and Greater Metropolitan Area: implications for public health and the public security agenda. *International Journal of Drug Policy* 49, 65–72.

US Department of State (2002). International narcotics control strategy report. Section IV: South America. Available at https://www.state.gov/ documents/organization/8695.pdf.

Weigert, M. A. (2010). *Uso de Drogas e Sistema Penal: Entre o Proibicion-ismo e a Redução de Danos*. Lumen Juris, Rio de Janeiro.

Wexler, D., and King, M. (2013). Promoting societal and juridical recep-tivity to rehabilitation: the role of therapeutic jurisprudence. In *Drug Treatment Courts: An International Response to Drug Dependent Offend-ers*. Organization of American States–CICAD/American University.

CHAPTER 5

Explaining the Failure of Drug Courts in the United Kingdom

By John Collins

This chapter offers an overview of the origins, evolution and ultimate collapse of drug courts in the United Kingdom (UK). Although remnants survive in Scotland, the model has largely disappeared from the legal landscape of England and Wales, despite a number of efforts to politically reinvigorate it. This chapter seeks to explain this failure. It is therefore focused on the institutional dynamics and actual operation of drug courts in the UK context, rather than serving as an exhaustive evaluation of the evidence on drug courts either globally or in the UK. It thereby represents a critical policy evaluation of the ultimate failure of drug courts to become established in a specific domestic environment despite strong political support. In so doing it attempts to highlight some of the structural reasons for the brief rise and quick collapse of the drug court model in England and Wales, in addition to an evaluation of the more fertile soil for drug courts found in Scotland and their eventual stasis/decline there as well. It thereby isolates some key socio-cultural and legal conditions that should, this chapter suggests, be part of the arithmetic of countries seeking to emulate this model around the world.

Many analyses point to international case studies, such as the US, and suggest that a more rigorous adherence to the authentic ideas or values inherent within the drug courts model would have rendered a more successful outcome in the UK (Donoghue, 2014; Jones and Kawalek, 2018). However, as James L. Nolan highlights, despite an often well-intentioned desire to spread interventions believed to hold a positive impact, '[e]mbedded in American problem-solving courts are cultural assumptions that significantly challenge long-held understandings of the meaning and practice of justice – assumptions that when transplanted /.../ may significantly challenge or alter the legal cultures of importing countries' (Nolan, 2009, p. 4). This insight has had major implications for the English experiment with, and ultimate abandonment of, the 'Dedicated Drug Court' (DDC). As this chapter reinforces, '[w]ithout a deeper understanding of the ongoing dialectic between law and culture, then, importers can underestimate the degree to which these programs carry with them' features of a foreign cultural context (Nolan, 2009, p. 4). Understanding this transfer and how it interacted with local legal and cultural contexts will, therefore, be a core focus of this chapter.

Further, this chapter questions the characterisation of DDCs as an inevitably 'softer' alternative to traditional criminal justice approaches. It suggests that the evidence from England paints an ambivalent picture, with some courts imposing more severe penalties on clients, while the quantitative evidence is either insufficient to draw conclusions or simply suggests a picture of failed institutional scale-up. As with the Dublin Drug Treatment Court in Ireland, UK drug courts appear to run into the fallacy of 'optimal expectations'. This produces an assumption of belief in their efficacy based on how they 'should' work, and 'would' work if functioning correctly, according to an abstract set of international principles (see, for example, Cooper et al., 2013). Further, it takes as an article of faith the underlying idea of court-based coercion (Tiger, 2013) as a self-evidently effective part of drug courts. As a result, this viewpoint holds: if aspiring models do not replicate the US model thoroughly they are inevitably pre-destined to failure. This view, however, runs counter to some of the wide literature looking at the outcomes of quasi-compulsory testing and treatment in UK and international contexts (McSweeney et al., 2008; Stevens et al., 2005).

This chapter suggests that the UK provides yet another example of an intervention that is imported from an extreme context – the US's War on Drugs – and imposed in an institutional, bureaucratic, cultural and social situation that ultimately 'rejects' the model. The

UK, including to a lesser extent Scotland, ultimately tells a story of a failed policy transfer from the US, despite prolonged periods of strong political support from the highest levels of government and many criminal justice organisations. Although perhaps well intentioned, the UK case tells a story of importing trains to a country with the wrong type of tracks. Ultimately, they will not connect with and run on the national infrastructure.

THE ORIGINS OF DRUG COURTS IN ENGLAND AND WALES

As with all other jurisdictions, the US models and evangelism from US proponents were leading catalysts for the creation of drug courts in the UK (Bean, 2002). Momentum towards England's first drug court model followed a series of visits to the US in the 1990s by UK officials. These included the then Chief Constable of the West Yorkshire police and the Assistant Director of Public Health of the Wakefield Health Authority at the time. The latter describes coming back 'a convert, a real enthusiast for what was happening there' (quoted in Nolan, 2009, p. 45). Two drugs courts were established under local initiative and with a mixture of local and private funds in West Yorkshire in mid-1998. These proved short-lived as a new UK-wide policy, the Drug Treatment and Testing Order (DTTO), was soon introduced. The DTTO consciously drew heavily on principles of the US drug court models, as McIvor writes:

> They allowed for the regular drug testing of offenders as a requirement of the court. Second, they emphasized the case management role of the supervising officer, who would be responsible for co-ordinating service provision rather than directly providing services. Third, and perhaps most significantly, they included provision for sentencers to take an active role in reviewing the progress of offenders on orders by bringing them back to court on a regular basis (or, alternatively, scrutinizing progress through paper-based reviews).
>
> (McIvor, 2009, p. 30)

The origin of the DTTO can be traced to a 1995 visit to the US by key UK officials. This visit ultimately translated into the creation of three pilot DTTO services by the New Labour government, under the 1998 Crime and Disorder Act (Nolan, 2009). These were in Gloucestershire, Liverpool and South London. The results were mixed and often poor. Recidivism rates were high and varied widely across pilots. Further, revocation rates were similarly high and again varied greatly, with one site showing a revocation rate of roughly 30% and another showing a rate of nearly 60% (Turnbull, 2000). Following the pilot, DTTOs were expanded to all 42 of Britain's probation services, absorbing the West Yorkshire courts and temporarily ending the idea of Britain having specific drugs courts. However, funding and operations were maintained for these drugs courts under the DTTO framework, even if their name formally changed (Nolan, 2009).

Generally, DTTOs were viewed as unsatisfactory in England and Wales for a variety of reasons, and this led to them being replaced. First was the lack of judicial continuity in the 'review hearings' (McSweeney *et al.*, 2008). Unlike US drug courts, where participants appear before the same judge throughout their programme, England and Wales has a system of Lay Magistrate Judges, a non-professional judiciary, which oversees the majority of criminal cases in England and Wales. The system of rotation accompanying this model resulted in clients facing different panels of magistrates throughout their programme. This factor made a judge-led case management approach close to impossible and ultimately handed power and responsibility to the probation officers involved. Further, the DTTOs were generally far more circumscribed in their powers than US drug court judges, removing a sense of a centralised coordinating mechanism for clients (Nolan, 2009). Similarly, 'performance management considerations' in England and Wales resulted in clients being driven before a judge to ensure 'timely' breach proceedings, rather than ensuring they appeared before the same judge (McSweeney *et al.*, 2008).

The Criminal Justice Act of 2003 phased out DTTOs as a standalone programme and incorporated components of them into a broader Community Order Scheme, which had a subservient Drug

Rehabilitation Requirement (DRR). Some highlighted the DRR as emerging with similar weaknesses, such as the 'performance management' culture, and thereby inevitably suffering many of the same weaknesses as the DTTO (McSweeney *et al.*, 2008). Simultaneously, scholars at the time questioned whether the UK was moving away from an approach to treatment based on self-motivation and 'volunteerism' and towards an ever more 'coercive' model of treatment. They argued this risked reversing

> the proven gains that have been produced by the earlier, voluntaristic approaches by diverting resources to more uncertain, coercive interventions. This has an evident opportunity cost that is being ignored and risks discouraging other drug users from entering and staying in treatment, it may divert staff from treatment modalities with better-known efficacy and may create perverse incentives to offend.   (Hunt and Stevens, 2004, p. 339)

Others viewed it as a general step forward in terms of embracing a more coherent US-style drug court model. As one commentator writes,

> Functioning in a fashion similar to that of DTTOs, DRRs can be tougher and more tailored to the specific circumstances of individual clients. Moreover, additional requirements, such as a curfew, residential restrictions, and mental health treatment, can be 'bolted on' to the DRR.   (Nolan, 2009, p. 46)

Despite this emerging top-down framework in England and Wales incorporating elements of US Drug Courts, local efforts continued to build a model based on even greater fidelity to the US approaches. Just eight months after the national implementation of the DRR, in 2005, new drug courts opened in West London and Leeds, again driven by the initiative of local judiciary (Nolan, 2009). One jurist in particular, Judge Justin Philips, became a strong evangelist for adapting UK judicial styles and culture to resemble US drug court 'theatre' as closely as possible (Nolan, 2009, p. 46).

More broadly, scholars highlight the emergence of the DTTO as a symptom of a key structural difference between the UK and US systems: the strength of the probation service. As Nolan writes, '[t]he DTTO and DRR programs are clearly led not by judges or magistrates but by probation officers', with some describing the DTTO as 'little more than a special type of probation order' (Nolan, 2009, p. 50). Some even concluded that drug courts faced institutional reticence because they posed a threat to the probation service, which risked being relegated in the process (Bean, 2002). This tension, similar to the tension between health and courts systems in the Dublin Drug Treatment Court, seemed evident in the 2011 Pilot evaluation of English and Welsh drug courts (Kerr *et al.*, 2011). On the one hand, DTTOs and DRRs witnessed a central and often unchallenged position for probation officers. On the other hand, the operation of the drug court pilots in the UK saw a conscious effort by some jurists to move the levers of control more towards the judge. As Judge Philips of the West London drug court commented, he would prefer to 'cut probation out', replacing them with treatment organisations as per the US system, as well as make it 'very much a judge-run court' (quoted in Nolan, 2009, p. 51).

Ultimately, six pilot DDCs began in magistrates' courts in England and Wales after 2004. First in 2005 in Leeds and London, with a further four introduced in Barnsley, Bristol, Cardiff and Salford in 2009. DDCs were viewed as a further extension of the DRR but one that more explicitly mimicked the US model in England and Wales (Kerr *et al.*, 2011, p. 1). The DRR represented one of 12 possible requirements available to English and Welsh courts as mechanisms to include in community sentences, enabling such things as mandatory periodic drug testing and the use of interim sanctioning. Building on these components, the DDC was intended as an integrated model that would in theory provide clearer structure to clients and better coordination across agencies (Kerr *et al.*, 2011).

A 2011 Pilot Evaluation of DDCs, conducted on behalf of the Ministry of Justice, held a limited scope and mandate for evaluation. It focused largely on mapping 'implementation, operation and core elements of the DDC model', but it was explicitly not aimed at measuring their 'impact in any way' (Kerr *et al.*, 2011, p. ii). As with official reviews of the Dublin Drug Treatment Court, the study found a receptive environment for the ideas underpinning DDCs, but overall a mixed picture of a model falling short of its optimal possibilities. If 'continuity of bench (magistrates or district judges)' could be achieved, if 'multiple agency presence' could be ensured, if 'quality treatment' was available, and if the model could be 'rolled out more widely', there was the chance, according to interviewees, to implement the model as 'a useful addition' to the range of initiatives aimed at reducing drug use and offending (Kerr *et al.*, 2011, p. 6). As with other cases examined in this book, the 'ifs' would prove critical.

Among the positives perceived by interview participants, the DDC could 'help to provide concrete goals, raise self-esteem, and provide a degree of accountability for offenders about their actions. DDCs were also seen as facilitating partnership between agencies' (Kerr *et al.*, 2011, p. iii). However, the evaluation called for national standardised training guidelines if the pilot was to be rolled out further as '[n]ew sites need clear guidance and support on how the model should be both theoretically and practically implemented' (Kerr *et al.*, 2011, p. iii). Importantly, the report highlights that its results were based largely on qualitative evidence and that the quality of the descriptive statistics and data used was low, thereby preventing clear extrapolations regarding 'the relationship between continuity of judiciary and breaches' (Kerr *et al.*, 2011, p. iii). It continued:

> The results from the quantitative analyses cannot be generalised beyond the pilot sites. This is because the representativeness of the pilot sample was not formally assessed, a large portion of information was missing, and sample sizes were often too low for the observed differences to be statistically significant.
>
> (Kerr *et al.*, 2011, p. 8)

The difficulty of conducting experiments within the criminal justice setting has been well highlighted in numerous other studies (McSweeney *et al.*, 2008). However, the reiteration of these central points in the English and Welsh cases clearly mitigate against straightforward assertions that drug courts simply 'work' (UNODC, 2005).

Meanwhile, the DDC models in England and Wales were explicitly built to address the weaknesses perceived within DTTOs and to a lesser extent the DRRs, although their legislative basis rested on DRRs. The key narratives to emerge from the pilot evaluation are mild enthusiasm in areas where the pilot ran, but also recognition of serious institutional and operational barriers. Far from the zealous pursuit of the drug court model throughout the US, for example, one finds a much more sober picture, one contingent on central government funding for dedicated roles. As staff highlighted in one case,

> If [we] didn't have a co-ordinators role we wouldn't have got off the ground with it /.../ you need somebody (a) to have that role assigned to them and (b) that's prepared to pick it up and do their best with it.   (Kerr *et al.*, 2011, p. 9)

Even when the dedicated coordinator was in place, one DDC was not fully operational for a further year, while funding for the role was transitional and only to support implementation and evaluation (Kerr *et al.*, 2011). Meanwhile the profile of clients suggests a homogenous group: mostly white (90%), mostly male, and with 45% of clients between the ages of 26 and 35. Although theft was the most common offence, at 40%, just under 25% of clients were involved for drug possession or cultivating cannabis, arguably an utterly pointless and counterproductive use of court services (Kerr *et al.*, 2011). Given the experience of other jurisdictions that have reported widespread 'cherrypicking' of drug court participants (Sevigny *et al.*, 2013), the ethnic and charge makeup of clients indicated a problematic selection criterion. Nevertheless, and again, the report noted that due to the poor 'quality of the data collected this may not be a true reflection of all cases going through' (Kerr *et al.*, 2011, p. 10).

Furthering the above, the lack of standardisation left significant problems for evaluation. The DDCs had varied entry points for individuals and saw conflicting views of whether DDC and non-DDC processes were more lenient in terms of sanctioning and their use of non-custodial sentencing. Further, narratives conflicted over whether magistrates, as lay amateurs relative to professional probation, solicitors and treatment providers, would heed the advice of the latter groups. Some interviewees suggested magistrates had largely been guided by the court professionals, a similar situation to that widely reported under the DTTO. Other interviewees suggested magistrates exerted their own judgement over court professionals, e.g. by imposing sentencing even against the recommendations of probation officers (Kerr *et al.*, 2011).

Similarly, levels of court formality varied across pilots. Nolan has written extensively on the cultural differences affecting the transfer of drug courts from the US to other jurisdictions, particularly the 'court as theatre' element (Nolan, 2009). Ireland and Scotland have explicitly rejected this approach for cultural reasons of 'reserve' and legal propriety (Butler, 2013; Nolan, 2009). England did witness some efforts to introduce a more informal court style, particularly in the West London drug court (Nolan, 2009). Overall, however, the adoption of the 'court as theatre' model was largely dependent on the individual judge or magistrates. For example, in some courts judiciary shook hands with clients. Others avoided crossing traditional lines. As one described it,

> From a magistrate's point of view, it can be quite difficult because we have to learn how informal to be /.../ it's all unwritten rules /.../ because we are breaking new ground with this.
>
> (Kerr *et al.*, 2011, p. 12)

Responses to breaches, or rule breaking by clients, were also found to be a mixed bag. The process was similar to, and under the same legislative basis as, any other court. Some of the staff interviewed believed the DDC treated clients in a more lenient manner, while other interviewees believed the DDC to be more punitive in its sanctioning than traditional courts. Some judges appeared to show greater leniency, while others overruled even parole officers' recommendations, arguing they, the judge, 'knew better' what the client needed. Accompanying this, the DDCs struggled to achieve judicial continuity and had less than clear impacts on the interaction between services, both of which the DDC was intended to foster. Both of these points raise questions of value added by the DDC, especially as interviewees suggested the interaction between services was already occurring prior to the establishment of the DDC (Kerr *et al.*, 2011).

The DDC itself was meant to be cost neutral, with the only central outlays being resources for a DDC coordinator to enable establishment, monitoring and evaluation. Some courts found the DDC encroaching on the space and time of other courts, however, as DRR outputs increased. Other courts languished with a lack of case work. Simultaneously, sites remained ambivalent about whether DDCs would increase the throughput of DRRs and thereby place stress on the existing court system at sites, with some suggesting they 'would struggle to provide this' (Kerr *et al.*, 2011, p. 20). As the 2011 pilot evaluation noted,

> The following developments were anticipated as necessary if numbers continued to rise: more court space and time for DDCs; a larger pool of magistrates; and potential staffing increases at treatment agencies and probation to cope with increased offender caseloads and extra time spent preparing reports and attending court.
>
> (Kerr *et al.*, 2011, p. 22)

In other words, to ensure that the DDC programme was effective, all wrap-around services would require additional resources and support to engage with the DDC. This logic arguably ran counter to the view that the DDC was being instituted to save on criminal justice system costs. Instead what emerges is a system that mimicked traditional courts but placed additional resource demands on systems already operating in some way alongside the court system, while producing results that were not clearly differentiated in terms of client outcomes. As the 2011 evaluation continued,

Isolating the perceived impacts of the DDC was difficult for offenders and staff. This was because other aspects of the process that were closely linked to the DDC model (such as the DRR or the involvement of services working with offenders) also contributed to achieving positive outcomes. A range of influences external to the operation of the DDC were also very significant. These included: individual offender motivation; the level of family support offenders received; the stability of their housing; and the quality and nature of the interventions they received. The part these external influences played on achieving offender outcomes, particularly motivation, cannot be underrated. Members of the judiciary, service staff and offenders alike concurred that DDC involvement itself was unlikely to result in positive outcomes without a degree of offender motivation, and this is where there was criticism of the drug court model for focusing resources on the courts rather than wider services.

(Kerr *et al.*, 2011, p. 23)

Overall, we find deep systemic tensions baked into the DDC at the outset, often only exacerbated rather than ameliorated by efforts to make the system more resemble a US drug courts model. On the one hand are traditional court and case management systems that had evolved practices and vested interests, while on the other was a desire to superimpose an ideal of hands-on judicial oversight and case management within the system. These tensions remained present throughout the English and Welsh experience with drug courts.

SCOTLAND

Scotland followed in Ireland's footsteps and undertook a lengthy consultation and review before launching its first drug court (see Chapter 3 on Ireland). The first court opened in Glasgow in late 2001, while an additional court opened in Fife in August 2002 (McIvor, 2009). Scotland's decision to trial the drug court model was directly influenced by US experiences, expertise and lobbying by groups such as the National Association of Drug Court Professionals (Nolan, 2009, p. 114). Overall, the Scottish Working Group adopted a cautious integrationist approach, which Bean has suggested involved rejecting the 'revolutionary features' of the US court models and their 'more extreme ideologies' (Bean, 2002, p. 1602). As an advocate for expanding drug courts in the UK, Bean commended the Working Group for retaining 'the spirit and procedures of its American parent but [ensuring they] are very Scottish in their approach' (Bean, 2002, p. 1605). The Working Group initially argued that drug courts could operate within existing legislative parameters, including the UK's DTTO scheme (Nolan, 2009, p. 114).

England and Wales soon moved beyond the unsatisfactory DTTO, replacing it with the DRR (see above). Nevertheless, Scotland found that the DTTO's implementation in Glasgow, beginning in 1999, and Fife, beginning in 2000, produced more positive results than were witnessed in England and Wales. They soon rolled the DTTO out to all regions of the country in 2003, the same year it was being wound down in England and Wales. The DTTO thereby continued to form the basis for Scottish drug courts (Nolan, 2009). Meanwhile, the Scottish Parliament expanded the scope of the drug courts to impose sanctions for minor 'compliance infractions', although it imposed upper limits on the sanctions. For example, a client could be sentenced to a maximum of 28 days in prison or 40 hours of community service on a specific order (Nolan, 2009, p. 122). The explicit reason for the limit was to prevent an 'unfair' outcome whereby a defendant could serve the original jail sentence and an additional sentence, thereby being 'punished twice' (Nolan, 2009, p. 124). This is a complaint that has been levelled against US drug courts (Csete and Tomasini-Joshi, 2015) and also, as this volume highlights, the Dublin Drug Treatment Court (see Chapter 3). Other reasons cited included the cost of short-term imprisonment and the likely exposure to drugs while there, along with a view that for 'high tariff' clients, jail may not serve as a marginal deterrent relative to other actions (Nolan, 2009, p. 124).

Nevertheless, similar to what was found with Canadian drug courts (Bakht, 2005), Scottish sheriffs proved reluctant to utilise sanctions, at least in the early stages (Nolan, 2009, p. 115). Meanwhile, Scotland maintained an overt and continued focus on preserving court formalities, due-process rights and the overall integrity of their court system (Nolan, 2009). As one Scottish drug court coordinator commented, 'judges really can do just about whatever they want, and I was a bit leery as to people's human rights', and as a result 'the procedural due process is very strictly adhered to' (Nolan, 2009, p. 127). In fact, it was their Irish colleagues who persuaded the Glasgow drug court planners to allow the sheriff (judge) to be present at the pre-court meeting. The Glasgow planners had worried it would represent a breach of due process as it may present inadmissible evidence, but their Dublin counterparts ultimately proved persuasive. However, on another point the Glasgow planners ignored the advice of the Dublin Drug Treatment Court. The latter, as highlighted in the Ireland chapter of this volume, explicitly excludes lawyers from proceedings (Nolan, 2009).

Whereas legal representatives in Dublin have agreed to stay out of the court, under the Scottish model, 'the legitimate role of the defence agent does not change in the drug court and includes that of advocacy, representing the interest of the client and safeguarding the rights of the defendant' (Fife Drug Court, 2002, p. 9). In another example, Nolan interviewed a Scottish sheriff who cited the European Convention of Human Rights as prohibiting him from making key decisions, such as imposing custodial sentences, without the defendant and his agent present (Nolan, 2009). This more cautious approach to legal processes runs counter to many assumed drug court practices outside Scotland whereby the client is excluded from key deliberative discussions. Further, a very reserved approach to intermediate sanctions is observed:

> Scottish sheriffs did not originally have the authority to impose a short-term jail sentence; they lacked the statutory authority to do so. When the Scottish Parliament eventually gave them this power, sheriffs were still very reluctant to use it.   (Nolan, 2009, p. 129)

Regarding principles and ideals of 'therapeutic justice', Scotland, like Ireland, largely ignores the philosophical cornerstone of the drug court model (Nolan, 2009, p. 131). One Scottish drug court worker interviewed suggested the idea of 'therapy' as anathema to Scottish treatment culture: 'we just don't have that /…/ It would never occur to us that people automatically need counselling to work through their issues' (quoted in Nolan, 2009, p. 133). Another goes further, arguing that the imposition of the American group model could prove damaging 'if you are going to get people to expose themselves emotionally /…/ we have to be careful that we don't damage them more than they already are damaged' (quoted in Nolan, 2009, p. 134). As the same interviewee states, '[the judge] does the law, we do the treatment' (quoted in Nolan, 2009, p. 134).

Similar to Ireland, the Scottish pilot lasted much longer than expected, and it was 2006 before the courts were extended beyond a pilot (Nolan, 2009). A key component to understand the Scottish development of, and continued enthusiasm for, drug courts may also be found in the process of devolution of powers from England, beginning with the elections to the new Scottish Parliament in May 1999. Drug courts coincided with the devolution of criminal justice powers and served as an early model to demonstrate a shift away from English modes. This political interaction was highlighted by the monopolisation of the issue by the Scottish National Party early on. Subsequently, the intervention garnered cross-party support: Nolan quotes one of the Glasgow drug court team as saying that 'the very fact that we have drug courts at all is an element of devolution' (Nolan, 2009, pp. 118–9).

THE COLLAPSE OF DRUG COURTS IN THE UK, 2013–PRESENT

Around 2013–14 drug courts went into a headlong decline in the UK. Although Scotland was seen as having a far more embedded and developed drug courts system, in 2013 the Fife Drug Court in Scotland closed, largely due to financial constraints (*Fife Today*, 2013). The Glasgow drug court continues with some suggestions of expansion (Jones and Kawalek, 2018). Meanwhile, in 2014 it became clear that other DDCs in the rest of the UK were slated for closure. As one official commented, despite vocal and widespread support among certain criminal justice reform groups, their collapse was 'all due to financial pressure'. He continued:

> It's a missed opportunity. There's no real data showing these courts have been successful and that has left an assumption they are not. There's no policy saying we are shutting them down. It's just happening by default and then it becomes standard that you don't have drug courts.   (Bowcott, 2014)

The West London DDC, a famed institution in the drug court literature (Nolan, 2009), underwent de facto closure following a funding cut. Meanwhile, on the broader problem-solving court front, the Liverpool Community Justice Centre also collapsed. Highlighting the less than stellar picture of the UK drug court experience, one worker in the West London court argued that the ultimate goal of the court was abstinence: 'We didn't do it that often but we did it more frequently than for people who didn't attend dedicated drug courts' (Bowcott, 2014). Despite the anecdotal claim, a joint paper by the New Economics Foundation and the Centre for Justice Innovation (CJI), the latter a strong advocate for problem-solving courts, tried to shed a positive light on the West London court. Ultimately, however, they acknowledged a lack of any research demonstrating the efficacy of the court in impacting recidivism rates (Estep, 2013). Central government, meanwhile, portrayed the issue as relating to decentralisation, with the then Justice Minister stating that the government was '[empowering] communities to support local initiatives' and that 'it will be for local communities to decide whether this approach is suitable for offenders in their area' (Bowcott, 2014).

In December 2015, a reprieve seemed imminent. Coinciding with the publication of a new report on problem-solving courts by the CJI, then Justice Secretary Michael Gove announced the creation of a working group on problem-solving courts (Bowcott, 2015). Seeking to reinvigorate support for the model at the time, Gove said:

> I recently visited the US to look at the innovative ways in which the judiciary were taking an active role in overseeing the rehabilitation of the offenders they had sentenced /.../ I was impressed by the potential of these 'problem-solving' courts to contribute to crime reduction and personal redemption.   (Quoted in Bowcott, 2015)

The CJI is a UK initiative of the US Center for Court Innovation, which was one of the early architects of US problem-solving courts, particularly the New York Red Hook Community Justice Center, which would become the US's 'flagship community court' (Nolan, 2009, p. 1). The 2015 CJI report argued that drug courts had a solid evidence base for reducing recidivism among certain groups, something broadly accepted in the international literature (Sevigny *et al.*, 2013), but acknowledged that this did not apply to juvenile drug courts, saying '[t]he evidence on juvenile drug courts is negative. It suggests they have either minimal or harmful impacts on young offenders' (Bowen and Whitehead, 2015, p. iii). As a result, the emphasis appeared to shift strongly towards family courts and other community-based interventions, rather than a specific linkage with drugs.

Gove's working group was to examine models of problem-solving courts and advise on the feasibility of possible pilots in England and Wales in 2016–17 (Webster, 2016). In May 2016, Cabinet supported the pilots. By October that year, however, Gove's replacement as Justice Secretary, Liz Truss, publicly lost interest and the initiative seemed 'in danger of losing momentum' (Bowcott, 2016a). The CJI authors became public advocates, arguing that

> There is a real opportunity to enable our criminal courts to contribute to cutting crime. The evidence for problem-solving courts is compelling – they work and are deliverable when set up in the right areas, with the right local judges and well-resourced treatment and rehabilitation services /.../ It is essential they have proper support from government and the senior judiciary. With our courts under unprecedented strain, problem-solving courts aren't a silver bullet but they offer a window of opportunity to cut crime, turn lives around and keep communities safer.   (Bowcott, 2016b)

By August 2016 it became apparent that the Justice Minister was deprioritising the initiative, with one inside official speculating: 'It appears that Liz Truss is sceptical. It looks too much like being nice to criminals and one of Michael Gove's "lovely ideas"' (Doward, 2016). An allusion to the seeming propensity of Gove to embrace idealised policies with vigour. Meanwhile, declining political support and funding saw the continued closure of problem-solving courts in England and Wales (Fouzder, 2018).

EVALUATING THE CAUSES OF FAILURE

In his 2002 paper, Philip Bean dissected the likelihood of drug courts taking root in the UK. He divided the 'obstacles', as he saw them, into manageable, 'evolutionary', ones versus three radical aspects that do not fit well with existing modes of the UK criminal justice system. These three radical aspects were:

1. The direct role of the judge in mandating and supervising a specific treatment regime. This is something widely criticised by public health experts as giving rise to many of the key abuses attributed to the US drug court model (Csete and Tomasini-Joshi, 2015). This level of supervision, Bean highlights, is not easily replicable in the UK system and is something that poses significant legislative barriers.
2. The 'team approach' of drug courts sidelines a basic tenet and protection of the adversarial system. Far from being an obstacle to the realisation of 'therapeutic justice' principles, this is intended to protect the offender from idiosyncratic decisions and corrupt practices in a system that holds an overwhelming power asymmetry over a client (Bean, 2002, p. 1599).
3. The punishment versus reward system, central to the US system and its underlying philosophy of 'addiction', requires the imposition of a novel idea for the British courts system: the use of 'multiple sanctions', something without clear precedent (Bean, 2002, p. 1599).

Nolan reinforced many of these obstacles and highlights, with the benefit of greater hindsight, a number of 'structural constraints' mitigating against a simple policy transfer from the US to the UK.

1. The use of Lay Magistrates in England.
2. The probation service as a powerful actor in the UK court system, in contrast to the US where it is a far less ubiquitous or tangible presence relative to the judge. For example, only 22% of drug courts in the US have a probation element (Nolan, 2009, pp. 50, 77).
3. Top-down versus bottom-up innovations. One key stimulant for the US drug court movement was the infusion of federal funds (McCoy, 2003, p. 1527), a process that has accelerated in response to the overdose crisis (Boghani, 2017). However, the models ultimately developed at local levels and retain a strong sense of independence. For example, when the Obama administration attempted to enforce acceptance of medication-assisted treatment such as methadone in 2015, the key lever was withholding federal funds from courts that refused (Department of Health and Human Services, 2015). Contrastingly, in England, legal innovations such as drug courts are more commonly initiated from the top, rather than at the local level, and are ultimately dependent on central government funding (Nolan, 2009). While Leeds and West London appear something of an early exception, they were ultimately enabled by national legislative changes around DTTOs, and subsequently driven by local zeal (Nolan, 2009).
4. Cultural divergence. Nolan cites a number of differences in how British and US courts might operate based on local culture. For example, 'public expressions of emotion', whereby judges in the US drug courts system hug and kiss participants, and court proceedings take place in a very public and often emotive and theatrical environment. Such displays and ideas have proven largely anathema to UK judicial protocol and styles, although some notable UK proponents have sought to sensitise the system to their ideas (Nolan, 2009, pp. 54–55). Others view the US's willingness to innovate as a positive example of modernising

outdated legal traditions. Simultaneously, this view holds that the UK's reticence derives from the 'stiff upper lip' mentality. Another possible explanation suggests that deep norms, such as the long democratic tradition in the UK as well as a view that protections within the European Union and the European Convention on human rights, represent developments towards a more therapeutic legal approach, thereby limiting the perceived need for local innovation (Jones and Kawalek, 2018).

5. Divergent treatment underpinnings. Although the US has undergone significant shifts in domestic drug policy under the Obama administration, the overarching thrust of the US drug court and treatment sectors has been, and remains, one geared towards abstinence rather than public-health-based harm reduction (Csete, 2016; Csete and Wolfe, 2017). In the UK courts, as elsewhere, 'harm reduction or reduced use is commonly viewed as success' (Nolan, 2009, p. 58), although an increasingly contested one in recent years as a 'recovery agenda' gained ground (Duke *et al.*, 2013; Wormer, 1999).

Perhaps added to this list might be the impact of austerity politics in the UK, and later the all-encompassing politics of Brexit. As the Conservative–Liberal Democrat coalition in 2010, through successive Conservative governments, embarked on a fiscal retrenchment through austerity, the scope for experimentation with new policies also shrank. This trend has simply been exacerbated by the UK's vote to leave the European Union in June 2016, which has prevented much appetite or bandwidth for policy experimentation within government (Jones and Kawalek, 2018).

CONCLUSION

The UK experience has numerous lessons. First, the difficulty of simple policy transfer of drug courts should never be underestimated in terms of institutional headwinds. McSweeney *et al.* write of this with a cautionary reminder of 'implementation failure' manifesting 'in the form of limited capacity and commitment amongst the various agencies involved to work together effectively in order to make the endeavour a viable one' (McSweeney *et al.*, 2008, p. 49). Although there is a frequent rhetorical refrain of adapting drug courts to local needs, the reality is much more complex and the odds of successful implementation are frequently weighted against novel interventions. The drug court model arose and sustained itself from a set of institutional circumstances in the US. Its role as a coordinating mechanism may not meet the circumstances or needs of the UK, and continued efforts to plant it may simply run into similar obstacles and failures.

Second, drug courts require resources. These can often be viewed as minimal in a context of establishing technical capacity but, as the case load grows, so too can the demand on other services that may not be optimally used within a drug court context. This soon raises significant questions of opportunity costs on top of the initial sunk costs associated with developing a drug court infrastructure in areas where other treatment priorities may be better served with the same resources.

What also emerges from the UK's navigations between DTTOs, DRRs and DDCs is the fundamental difference between incorporating aspects of drug treatment modalities and wrap-around services within existing criminal justice system responses, versus importing a 'radical' model of activist judicial practice. What one generally sees in England and Wales is an initiative aimed at a more structured approach to case management within the courts. Within this we find an extremely ambivalent picture on day-to-day operational aspects, coupled with a larger systemic picture of ultimate rejection of the model. DDCs were expected to be simultaneously reactive and reflective of local needs while attempting to implement national and centrally determined social service and court programmes. The DDCs' failure to take root within this policy paradox was perhaps both predetermined and predictable. Further, the inescapable incongruence between a magistrate system and a therapeutic justice model based on judicial continuity is simply not one that can be overcome without a major adjustment to the criminal justice system in England and Wales.

Ultimately, the constant need to navigate and overcome the, often-contradictory, goals of local innovators versus central government priorities, perhaps more than any other factor, explains the ultimate unsustainability of drug courts in a UK context. Although some drug courts emerged at a local level, the driving actors ultimately found themselves hostage to the whims and changing tides of central government priorities, funding and standardisation of procedures and legislative practice. No level of local enthusiasm for, or belief in, the ideas of therapeutic justice can bridge the fundamental need to secure central government funds and coalesce highly centralised service provision around a new policy innovation. Further, this is all in the face of deeply entrenched institutional interests, each with its own funding needs and incentives. Couple these constraints with a conservative court system, not calibrated for a lengthy case management approach, and one finds a perhaps predictable recipe for failure in the UK. Although Scotland, England and Wales appeared to diverge at one point, they eventually returned to a similar position of finding these models unsustainable in the long run, even with the support of key top-level government figures. The lessons of the UK's failed experiments with drug courts, thus far, provide a cautionary tale to other governments embarking on the model. Even with the best intentions to adapt and embed the model in different legal, cultural and social backgrounds than the US context that birthed it, success is far from guaranteed, or even likely.

BIBLIOGRAPHY

Bakht, N. (2005). Problem solving courts as agents of change. *Criminal Law Quarterly* 50, 224–254.

Bean, P. (2002). Drug treatment courts, British style: the drug treatment court movement in Britain. *Substance Use & Misuse* 37, 1595–1614 (https://doi.org/10.1081/JA-120014423).

Boghani, P. (2017). Trump's opioid commission recommends drug courts. How do they work? *PBS News*, available at https://www.pbs.org/wgbh/frontline/article/trumps-opioid-commission-recommends-drug-courts-how-do-they-work/ (accessed 26 May 2018).

Bowcott, O. (2014). Why are special courts that can help drug users at risk of being scrapped? *The Guardian*, available at https://www.theguardian.com/society/2014/jun/10/drug-courts-risk-being-scrapped   (accessed 5 July 2018).

Bowcott, O. (2015). MoJ considers specialist courts for issues such as domestic abuse. *The Guardian*.

Bowcott, O. (2016a). US-style problem solving courts plan losing momentum, says legal charity. *The Guardian* (Society), available at https://www.theguardian.com/society/2016/oct/12/us-style-problem-solving-courts-plan-losing-momentum-says-legal-charity (accessed 2 July 2018).

Bowcott, O. (2016b). US-style problem-solving courts planned for England and Wales. *The Guardian*.

Bowen, P., and Whitehead, S. (2015). Problem-solving courts: an evidence review. Centre for Justice Innovation, London.

Butler, S. (2013). The symbolic politics of the Dublin drug court: the complexities of policy transfer. *Drugs: Education, Prevention and Policy* 20, 5–13.

Cooper, C. S., Chisman, A. McG., and Lomba Maurandi, A. (eds) (2013). *Drug Treatment Courts: An International Response for Drug Dependent Offenders*. OAS–American University, Washington, DC.

Csete, J. (2016). Public health research in a time of changing drug policy: possibilities for recovery? In *After the Drug Wars: Report of the LSE Expert Group on the Economics of Drug Policy* (edited by Collins, J., and Soderholm, A.). LSE IDEAS, London.

Csete, J., and Tomasini-Joshi, D. (2015). Drug courts: equivocal evidence on a popular intervention. New York. Available at https://www.opensocietyfoundations.org/reports/drug-courts-equivocal-evidence-popular-intervention.

Csete, J., and Wolfe, D. (2017). Seeing through the public health smokescreen in drug policy. *International Journal of Drug Policy* 43, 91–95 (https://doi.org/10.1016/j.drugpo.2017.02.016).

Department of Health and Human Services (2015). Grants to expand substance abuse treatment capacity in adult and family drug courts. Available at https://www.samhsa.gov/sites/default/files/grants/pdf/ti-15-002-modified-due.pdf (accessed 3 August 2017).

Donoghue, J. (2014). *Transforming Criminal Justice? Problem-Solving and Court Specialisation*. Routledge, London.

Doward, J. (2016). Liz Truss abandons Gove's plan for problem-solving courts. *The Observer*.

Duke, K., Herring, R., Thickett, A., and Thom, B. (2013). Substitution treatment in the era of 'recovery': an analysis of stakeholder roles and policy windows in Britain. *Substance Use & Misuse* 48, 966–976 (https://doi.org/10.3109/10826084.2013.797727).

Estep, B. (2013). *Better Courts Case-Study: West London Drug Court*. New Economics Foundation, London.

Fife Today (2013). Fife drug court to close. *Fife Today*, available at https://www.fifetoday.co.uk/news/fife-drug-court-to-close-1-2889458.

Fouzder, M. (2018). 'Pennies' will save pioneering court unit. *Law Society Gazette*, available at https://www.lawgazette.co.uk/news/pennies-will-save-pioneering-court-unit/5066612.article (accessed 2 July 2018).

Hunt, N., and Stevens, A. (2004). Whose harm? Harm reduction and the shift to coercion in UK drug policy. *Social Policy and Society* 3, 333–342 (https://doi.org/10.1017/S1474746404001964).

Jones, E., and Kawalek, A. (2018). Dissolving the stiff upper lip: opportunities and challenges for the mainstreaming of therapeutic jurisprudence in the United Kingdom. *International Journal of Law and Psychiatry*, posted online 8 July (https://doi.org/10.1016/j.ijlp.2018.06.007).

Kerr, J., Tomkins, C., Tomaszewski, W., Dickens, S., Grimshaw, R., Wright, N., and Barnard, M. (2011). The dedicated drug courts pilot evaluation process study. Ministry of Justice Research Series, No. 1/11. Ministry of Justice, London.

McCoy, C. (2003). The politics of problem-solving: an overview of the origins and development of therapeutic courts. *American Criminal Law Review* 40(4), 1513–1534.

McIvor, G. (2009). Therapeutic jurisprudence and procedural justice in Scottish drug courts. *Criminology & Criminal Justice* 9, 29–49 (https://doi.org/10.1177/1748895808099179).

McSweeney, T., Stevens, A., Hunt, N., and Turnbull, P. J. (2008). Drug testing and court review hearings: uses and limitations. *Probation Journal* 55, 39–53 (https://doi.org/10.1177/0264550507085678).

Nolan, J. L. (2009). *Legal Accents, Legal Borrowing: The International Problem Solving Court Movement*. Princeton University Press, Princeton, NJ.

Sevigny, E. L., Fuleihan, B. K., and Ferdik, F. V. (2013). Do drug courts reduce the use of incarceration? A meta-analysis. *Journal of Criminal Justice* 41, 416–425 (http://dx.doi.org/10.1016/j.jcrimjus.2013.06.005).

Stevens, A., Berto, D., Heckmann, W., Kerschl, V., Oeuvray, K., Ooyen, M., Steffan, E., and Uchtenhagen, A. (2005). Quasi-compulsory treatment of drug dependent offenders: an international literature review. *Substance Use & Misuse* 40, 269–283 (https://doi.org/10.1081/JA-200049159).

Tiger, R. (2013). *Judging Addicts: Drug Courts and Coercion in the Justice System (Alternative Criminology)*. NYU Press.

Turnbull, P. J. (2000). Drug treatment and testing orders: final evaluation report. Home Office, London.

UNODC (2005). Drug treatment courts work! United Nations Office on Drugs and Crime, Vienna.

Webster, R. (2016). The evidence on problem-solving courts. Available at http://www.russellwebster.com/evidence-problem-solving-courts/.

Wormer, K. V. (1999). Harm induction vs. harm reduction: comparing American and British approaches to drug use. *Journal of Offender Rehabilitation* 29, 35–48 (https://doi.org/10.1300/J076v29n01_03).

CHAPTER 6

Diversion in the Criminal Justice System: Examining Interventions for Drug-Involved Offenders

By Winifred Agnew-Pauley

The criminal justice system (CJS) routinely deals with drug-related crime and offenders. This includes a wide spectrum of offenders, such as (1) individuals charged with using or possessing illicit drugs; (2) individuals who have problematic drug use, or are dependent on the use of drugs, and/or use criminal means as a way to procure drugs; (3) individuals who are involved in the sale or trafficking of drugs; and (4) individuals who fall into more than one or all of these categories. Individuals involved in drugs and crime have varying levels of needs within the CJS, particularly those whose offending behaviour is directly linked to illicit drug use. Criminal justice systems internationally have gradually adapted to recognise the inefficiency and ineffectiveness of dealing with drug-related crime through traditional justice mechanisms and have begun acknowledging the complex relationship between drugs and crime (Longshore *et al.*, 2001; Lutze and van Wormer, 2014). To address these issues a wide range of responses and interventions have evolved. The overarching aim of these interventions has been to seek alternative ways of dealing with drug-involved offenders that result in more positive outcomes at the individual and community level.

Such interventions are known as diversion programmes. These programmes are characterised as any intervention that re-routes offenders away from traditional criminal justice processing and/or encourages participation in alternative programmes or services. Diversion can be used for various offending groups, such as individuals who use drugs, young people and individuals with mental health issues. This review will focus on drug-related diversion programmes. The motivations for implementing diversion programmes are varied and wide-ranging, including, for example, introducing a greater emphasis on public health outcomes; addressing the stigma associated with, and the criminogenic influence of, formal contact with the CJS; lessening the burden on criminal justice resources, such as overcrowded prisons; and improving the cost-effectiveness of the CJS (Clancey and Howard, 2006; Prichard, 2010; Shanahan *et al.*, 2017b). Referrals that come through the CJS are also an increasingly important route for services to identify and make contact with prospective clients and for individuals to access these services, particularly in the case of hard-to-reach populations (Hayhurst *et al.*, 2015).

Diversion programmes have existed both formally and informally for some time, ranging from early youth courts to informal police warnings or cautions. It is important to note that police routinely 'divert' potential offenders from the CJS through the exercise of police discretion, particularly drug-related offenders for minor infractions (Baker and Goh, 2004). However, over time these mechanisms have become more formalised, regulated and codified into policy and legislation (Bull, 2005). This has had a broad range of implications, yet has largely represented a positive shift towards the adoption of alternative procedures for engaging with people who use drugs and a recognition of the inefficiencies of the CJS in absorbing large numbers of individuals with complex social needs and health issues.

Drug diversion was initially met with some resistance from policymakers and law enforcement for being a 'soft' option, in a political climate where being 'tough on crime', and therefore 'tough on drugs', has generally prevailed (Hughes, 2007). However, the expansion and proliferation of drug diversion programmes in the United Kingdom (UK), the United States (US), Australia and many other countries (Bull, 2003) suggests diversion has withstood initial resistance despite entrenched political ideas and rhetoric. Recognising this climate, the initial implementations of drug diversion programmes, for example the Illicit Drug Diversion Initiative introduced in Australia in 1999, were framed as maintaining 'the structures of the criminal law, but [offering] drug users a second chance' (Hughes, 2007, p. 364). Beneath this framing remained a recognition that viewing drug diversion programmes purely as drug use and crime reduction mechanisms neglected their potential for broader social impact. In fact, drug diversion that is premised purely on the reduction of drug use or crime may 'increase the likelihood of harm and be counterproductive' (Hughes, 2007, p. 364).

Internationally, growing support for diversion programmes coincided with a recognition of the need to address drug use and drug-related crime as a broader social issue:

> Diversion should be seen as initiating the process of social change, rather than simply treating 'drug problems'. Good diversion practice will recognise the interplay of various social issues, e.g. employment, finance, health, legal etc. and will engage, where appropriate, a whole range of support services to address them.
>   (Alcohol and Other Drugs Council of Australia, 1996, n.p.)

This chapter will critically examine drug diversion in the CJS to address the questions of what can be understood by the term 'drug diversion' within the CJS, and what the key lessons are from existing experiences and research. The chapter will begin by outlining the complex relationship between drug use and crime before going on to define drug diversion, drawing on the two key theoretical concepts of true diversion and therapeutic jurisprudence. It will outline the different types of diversion programmes at different stages of the CJS, and the principles of best practice within drug diversion. The limitations of existing diversion research will then be discussed, including a discussion of net-widening and the methodological challenges involved in programme evaluation. The final section will draw conclusions and implications for practice.

RELATIONSHIP BETWEEN DRUG USE AND CRIME

Understanding the policy response to drug-related crime necessitates an understanding of the relationship between drugs and crime: a topic that has received significant scholarly attention (Seddon, 2000; McSweeney *et al.*, 2007; Bennett, 2009). Contrary to many media and public discourses that suggest a linear and clear link between drug use and crime, researchers have long stressed the importance of appreciating the complexities of this relationship (Hucklesby and Wincup, 2010).

A number of key points permeate the research in this area.

- The vast majority of people who use drugs do not suffer from disorders related to drug use, and as such do not require treatment (United Nations Office on Drugs and Crime [UNODC], 2014).
- Not all drug users will commit crime, and the punishment of crime alone is therefore unlikely to reduce drug use; similarly, drug treatment alone is unlikely to directly reduce crime (Seddon, 2000).
- Distinctions between users (e.g. recreational and dependent users) are often misunderstood, where population studies of casual users find 'little relationship to crime' (Lilley, 2017, p. 679).
- A smaller number of offenders with persistent and severe drug use and offending behaviour tend to commit a larger proportion of crime. These persistent offenders are more likely to be resistant to treatment and to be disillusioned by repeated CJS interaction (Bull, 2003).
- The subset of offenders who reoffend often have significantly more complex needs: for example, they are more likely to be drug dependent, unemployed, less educated and have more health problems (Shanahan *et al.*, 2017a).

Evidence from research on the drug–crime nexus suggests that 'drug use and criminality may develop in parallel, perhaps via a third factor such as socioeconomic deprivation' (Hayhurst *et al.*, 2015, p. 2).

Developing alternative approaches for re-routing offenders who use drugs away from traditional criminal justice processes represents a vital acknowledgment of the complexity of these issues and of the underlying causes of drug use and crime. Such programmes recognise that 'drug use as a determinant of crime blames individuals at the expense of wider social policy' (Clancey and Howard, 2006, pp. 377–378) and the need to adopt a social approach towards drug use and crime, as opposed to a strictly criminal justice approach. Diversion programmes for drug-involved offenders place a greater emphasis on redressing social factors (such as education, unemployment or housing) and take into account the varying needs of this group, while also addressing the inefficiencies of overburdened criminal justice systems.

DEFINING DIVERSION

Diversion has multiple context-specific meanings. At a broad level, diversion encompasses any form of re-routing of offenders who use drugs 'who would otherwise be convicted and penalized through the traditional criminal justice process and includes the re-routing of such offenders at any stage of the criminal justice process' (Expert Working Group of the UN International Drug Control Program, 1999; cited in Bull, 2003, p. 10). The main theoretical concepts underpinning drug diversion programmes are true diversion, therapeutic jurisprudence and harm reduction. These approaches differ in their rationale, 'to either minimise the harmful effects of formal criminal justice interventions or to provide opportunities to address drug use/offending' (Hughes *et al.*, 2014, p. 10).

True diversion within the CJS, in the purest, criminological sense of the term, involves diverting or re-routing an offender out of the system entirely, with no subsequent contact or consequence. This would mean that an individual would not receive treatment, be granted access to programmes or services, or receive any further follow up from the CJS. In practice, diversion focuses more on *minimising* the level of contact with, or the extent of penetration of, the CJS, and as such takes an approach that is less punitive than what would otherwise have applied (Wundersitz, 2007).

Therapeutic jurisprudence is a theory that considers the law as a 'social force that produces behaviours and consequences' (Wexler, 2000, p. 125). It places greater emphasis on taking advantage of the moment individuals are brought into the CJS as an opportunity to have a positive impact on individual well-being and shifts the role of the CJS from adversarial to problem-solving, leading to more active participation in the rehabilitation of offenders (Wundersitz, 2007). Birgden summarises the main principles of therapeutic jurisprudence:

> First, the way the law is implemented and operates can either increase, decrease, or have a neutral effect on psychological well-being. Social scientists should identify laws, processes and procedures that enhance wellbeing. Second, the law should capitalise on the moment that offenders are brought before it as a way to start pro-social lifestyles. Third, the law should be a multidisciplinary endeavour with the relationship between law and psychology being cooperative rather than antagonistic. Therapeutic jurisprudence utilises social science knowledge to determine ways in which the law can enhance psychological wellbeing. Fourth, the law balances community protection (i.e. justice principles) against individual autonomy (i.e. therapeutic principles) and legal considerations such as individual autonomy and community safety should not be trumped.   (Birgden, 2002, p. 182)

Understanding diversion through a therapeutic jurisprudence lens places greater emphasis on re-routing offenders into a programme or service, and for criminal justice, health and social services to play an active and engaged role in rehabilitating the individual. Critiques of therapeutic jurisprudence suggest that in taking a more active role, the criminal justice system risks overstepping its legal authority and infringing on the rights of the individual through a potential erosion of due process and the adversarial system (Nolan, 2010). The application of therapeutic jurisprudence varies by context. Drug courts in Australia, for example, accept therapeutic jurisprudence as the underpinning philosophy. However, judges take a critically reflective approach to its application. This means that while they advocate the role of the court in encouraging pro-social outcomes, they defend the importance of the judiciary in ensuring that court-based interventions do not overstep their legal parameters. As Nolan argues (commenting on problem-solving courts in Australia and Canada),

> While they embrace therapeutic jurisprudence, judicial officials in Australia and Canada /.../ show greater restraint than is generally demonstrated in American problem-solving courts. Relatedly, both countries show more concern for the protection of offenders' due process rights and the preservation of the dignity of the court. Particularly in Australia, there is considerable evidence of critical reflection about the potential hazards or harmful consequences of these court programs.   (Nolan, 2009, p. 77)

Therapeutic jurisprudence differs to the understanding of 'true diversion', where greater emphasis is placed on diverting an individual away from the CJS and minimising further contact with the CJS altogether.

Many scholars argue that diversion must also be underpinned by a commitment to harm reduction. They contend that drug diversion programmes that fixate solely on reducing drug use and crime, as opposed to improving broader social outcomes, can prove counterproductive and increase societal harms (Hughes, 2007). For some this is embodied by a shift towards 'problem solving justice', whereby 'classical theories of crime and punishment have evolved through post-welfare penological thought into, finally, the harm-minimisation philosophy that has culminated in the concepts of diversionary justice and problem-oriented courts' (Cappa, 2006, p. 146). Others have rejected this 'problem solving justice' approach as applied to drug-involved offenders as simply a continuation of coercive modalities that pose fundamental issues about free will, agency and the right to health (Tiger, 2013; Csete and Tomasini-Joshi, 2015).

Diversion in practice within the CJS incorporates different elements of the definition and underpinning theories and therefore has a dual function: first, to *divert away* from the CJS via an alternative procedure to traditional criminal justice processing; and second, to *divert into* programmes or services aimed at addressing drug use and offending behaviour, as well as other social outcomes (Hughes and Ritter, 2008; Hughes *et al.*, 2014). Adopting one approach without the other can be problematic. Simply diverting away from criminal justice procedures can 'avoid unnecessary intervention and can increase the efficiency of the CJS, but /.../ may not address the causes of problematic drug use or offending', thus 'introducing a therapeutic component, in diverting an offender into a programme, can increase the potential of addressing the underlying causes of drug use and crime' (Hughes and Ritter, 2008, p. 5). Balancing diversion, therapeutic jurisprudence and harm reduction can vary depending on where programmes occur along the criminal justice continuum (Wundersitz, 2007), or programmes can incorporate elements of the different theoretical underpinnings.

TYPES OF DIVERSION

Diversion can occur at multiple stages throughout the CJS continuum and can broadly be divided into police or court-based interventions. Police diversions, or front-end diversions, can occur at any time while the police are in contact with an offender. This can be pre-arrest, once an offence has been detected but no charges have been laid (e.g. a caution or a fine), or post-arrest prior to the matter being heard in court, while the offender is either in custody or awaiting trial (e.g. arrest referral schemes or treatment as a condition of bail). Some examples of commonly used police-led diversions are cannabis cautioning schemes or diversion into drug education programmes, for example in Australia (Baker and Goh, 2004; Shanahan *et al.*, 2017a) (see Chapter 2), and the arrest referral schemes in the UK (Hunter *et al.*, 2005; Hayhurst *et al.*, 2015). Arrest referral schemes are an example of diversion following the point of arrest, whereby offenders who are in police custody are offered the opportunity to be assessed by an independent drug specialist who can refer them into treatment services. Importantly, participation in the UK schemes are voluntary, and the scheme does not offer an alternative to prosecution (Hunter *et al.*, 2005).

Court-led interventions can occur pre-plea, where an offender's case has been heard at trial but no plea has been entered; post-plea, where a plea has been entered but sentencing is delayed; or post-sentence, where participation in a programme replaces or is part of the sentence. Court-led diversion interventions are largely dominated by drug courts. A drug court is a specialist court, or a problem-solving court, that aims to divert offenders whose drug use is considered to be the underlying cause of criminal offending into drug treatment, as opposed to traditional criminal sanctioning or incarceration. While specific programme components vary between individual drug courts and jurisdictions, the main elements of a drug court typically involve participation in court-mandated drug treatment, intensive case management, regular drug testing, a formalised system of rewards and sanctions to encourage compliance, and regular contact with a drug court judge (Longshore *et al.*, 2001; Lilley, 2017).

Diversion programmes vary in the outcomes or services they offer as part of participation. This can range from offering offenders a warning or fine (in the place of arrest or a criminal conviction), a referral to drug education services, youth conferencing, access to social services such as employment or housing support, intensive case management, treatment for drug dependence (with varying degrees of intensity from non-residential to residential) or supervision by a law enforcement, health or social service professional (Hughes and Ritter, 2008). Proponents argue that best-practice programmes ought to be responsive to individual needs, with a range of service referral options available.

Diversion interventions also target different categories of offences and offenders. These range from minor offences to more serious offences and can include both drug offences and drug-related offences (non-drug offences that are linked to drug use). The intensity of the diversionary response varies depending on where it is initiated in the criminal justice continuum, where police diversion initiatives are at the lower end of the spectrum and court-based initiatives are at the higher end of the spectrum. Police diversions aim to divert offenders at an early stage of criminal justice processes, with the aim of minimising further contact with the CJS. These front-end responses therefore have a low intensity of supervision and minimal conditions for compliance and further follow up, and they are therefore most closely aligned with the criminological concept of diversion (Wundersitz, 2007). Alternatively, court-based interventions (such as drug courts) are initiated at a much later stage in the criminal justice process and involve a much higher intensity of supervision, conditions of compliance and consequences for perceived failure to comply. The entrenched positioning of drug courts within the CJS (occurring after arrest and charge, and most often including a requirement of a guilty plea) prevents them from offering a pure form of diversion: 'at best, they provide an alternative method of processing and /…/ the possibility of a less severe penalty, including the potential to avoid imprisonment' (Wundersitz, 2007, p. 32). Matching the severity of the offence and drug use behaviour to the appropriate diversionary response is an integral part of effective diversion.

Different countries take different approaches to implementing diversion programmes. These range from a formalised, centralised system of programmes governed by legislation and monitored by the government ('top down') to a 'bottom-up' approach characterised by local initiatives and grassroots advocacy. The Australian approach to diversion, for example, is operated through a fairly centralised system via initiatives at both the state and federal level; however, programmes vary by state. The Australian approach to diversion is to operate with a broad system of diversionary measures across the criminal justice spectrum, where court-based interventions (i.e. drug courts) are seen as a last resort (Freiberg *et al.*, 2016). This differs to the US system of diversion, which largely relies on drug courts as the predominant diversion response. While other drug diversion programmes do exist in the US, they are often built into, or are part of, an existing drug court programme (Bull, 2003). In contrast to the Australian system, the US approach takes more of a bottom-up approach, driven by a strong movement of drug court professionals and drug court judges. The US approach places much greater emphasis on judge-supervised drug treatment and uses drug courts as a mechanism to target a wide range of offenders, including those involved in recreational or minor drug use (Lilley, 2017).

BEST PRACTICE FOR DRUG DIVERSION PROGRAMMES

Several programme evaluations and government discussion papers have attempted to identify best-practice guidelines in the delivery of diversion programmes in the CJS. These have included both overarching guidelines for all diversion programmes, for example the *Principles of Best Practice in Drug Diversion Programmes* (1996) by the Alcohol and Other Drug Council of Australia, and guidelines for specific programmes. Examples of the latter include *Ten Key Components of Drug Courts* (1997) by the National Association of Drug Court Professionals and *Arrest Referral: A Guide to Principles and Practice* by Russell and Davidson (2002). Most of these guidelines were developed to assist in the initial establishment of diversion initiatives, and as such were not necessarily based on empirical evidence as none was yet available. Reviewing the original diversion guidelines and the emergent evaluation literature that has been conducted on diversion programmes (Bull, 2005), a number of consistent themes emerge, in relation to programme design, delivery, operation and monitoring.

Programme design

Many argue that the design of diversion programmes should be underpinned by a sound programme philosophy and a commitment to the theoretical foundations of diversion. This has been enumerated as a commitment to diversion through alternate mechanisms to the CJS, therapeutic jurisprudence and harm reduction. Programmes should have clear eligibility criteria for participants to ensure they are carefully selected, and ideally should follow the risk–need–responsivity principle, whereby an individual's level of need and their risk of future offending is matched to an appropriate programme responsive to their circumstances (Reich *et al.*, 2018). Diversion programmes also must be accessible to all those who are eligible, irrespective of the nature of their substance use, their age, gender, cultural background, place of residence or economic status (Bull, 2005).

Identification of individual needs and the referral process ought to be efficient and effective. Similarly, particularly for more intensive programmes, such as drug courts, there needs to be 'early identification of individuals who are likely to be terminated from the program so that more appropriate alternatives can be provided' (Wundersitz, 2007, p. 112).

Importantly, diversion programmes must always uphold the rights of the offender, and participation in programmes must be based on informed consent. As an alternative to the CJS, diversion programmes must not be more intrusive, intensive or severe than the traditional criminal justice response (Wundersitz, 2007; Hughes and Ritter, 2008). Diversion programmes should also include a built-in system of social support that includes access and referral to a range of social services including (but not limited to) drug treatment, education, employment services, housing and other forms of social support – these services should also include a follow-up component, where participants are supported as needed after programme completion (Bull, 2005).

Programme delivery

The effective delivery of diversion programmes necessitates coordination and collaboration between all agencies involved. At the core of diversion programmes is a partnership between the health and criminal justice sectors, maintained through effective communication, management and governance. Partnerships need to be genuinely equal, without allowing the CJS to be a dominant partner, to ensure that harm reduction and health-related goals are on an equal basis with crime reduction and law enforcement goals. This has often proved hard to achieve, as with all governmental coordination efforts between departments and power centres with often divergent needs and interests, but it is key for attempting to employ a comprehensive service approach to diversion clients (Hunter *et al.*, 2005).

Programme operation

The effective operation of diversion programmes requires political support and secure funding. Specific legislation or policy is a key way for diversion programmes to ensure programme longevity and fidelity, as well as to ensure that interventions do not depend on the discretion of law enforcement or judicial officers. Sufficient and sustained funding allocated to all aspects of the diversion programme, including training of involved parties and programme evaluations, is essential. Furthermore, effective service provision is vital, particularly in relation to drug treatment programmes. Programmes with poor-quality treatment are unlikely to work, nor will programmes that are too punitive in their approach. As with all treatment services, participants introduced into services with limited space or long waiting lists will struggle to achieve intended outcomes (Andrews *et al.*, 1990; Social Science Research Council, 2018).

Compliance mechanisms are also widely viewed as a key component of diversion programmes (Cooper *et al.*, 2013), although scholars differ over the philosophical and evidentiary basis for repeated sanctioning (Csete and Tomasini-Joshi, 2015). For example, many drug court practitioners argue that appropriate and consistent sanctions should be in place for those who do not comply. However, these must be balanced to ensure they are no more intrusive than a criminal justice response and do not produce perverse sentencing outcomes (Sevigny *et al.*, 2013).

Programme monitoring

Diversion programmes are monitored in two ways: participants within the programme are monitored to ensure compliance and the programme itself is monitored to ensure it is achieving its intended aims. For participants, appropriate and consistent sanctions should be sufficient to encourage compliance but must not outweigh the overall response of the programme (in terms of being no more intrusive than a traditional criminal justice response) (Bull, 2005). In terms of the diversion programme itself, there must be an ongoing commitment to monitoring and evaluation. This means ensuring that programme data is collected and shared and evaluations are robust and independent (see below).

These principles, relating to programme design, delivery, operation and monitoring, have been considered as best-practice guidelines. The link, however, is tentative given that more recent guidelines have not yet been developed and evaluations of diversion programmes have been methodologically weak (Cooper *et al.*, 2013). For individuals, diversion programmes can reduce drug use and criminal behaviour, as well as improve other social outcomes such as physical health, mental health, employment prospects and personal relationships. At the community level, diversion programmes can lead to less crime in the community and effective partnerships between health, criminal justice and social service agencies (Bull, 2003). Diversion programmes have also been shown to improve relationships between law enforcement and the community, and more positive perceptions of police legitimacy (Shanahan *et al.*, 2017b). For the CJS, diversion programmes reduce the burden on criminal justice resources and can be significantly more cost-effective (Baker and Goh, 2004; Shanahan *et al.*, 2017a).

For diversion programmes to achieve these outcomes, it is important to note that best-practice guidelines can be difficult to implement and operationalise. The uptake and roll-out of programmes can take longer than expected and initial take-up rates can be low (Bull, 2003). Furthermore, most extant evaluation outcomes and impacts generally stem from individual programmes, to varying degrees, and some diversion programmes have shown more positive results than others. While best-practice principles have been found to be supported by evaluations of diversion programmes and have been shown to lead to some (though not necessarily all) of these individual and community impacts, more research, as well as updated programme guidelines, is needed that evaluates single programmes as well as systems of diversion programmes that is based on robust research methodologies.

LIMITATIONS OF DIVERSION

Diversion programmes have the potential to produce promising outcomes for both individuals and communities. However, it is important to consider the limitations of these interventions.

Methodological weakness

Evaluations of diversion programmes have often been limited in scope, with poor methodological quality and a heavier focus on drug courts as the main diversion programme for drug offending, with less attention given to other diversion programmes (see Chapter 1).

Systematic reviews and meta-analyses in this field frequently result in high levels of heterogeneity, meaning that study designs and outcomes are too diverse to draw conclusions from (Schwalbe *et al.*, 2012; Hayhurst *et al.*, 2015), and methodological weakness from poor-quality research designs is consistently found as a recurring outcome (Mitchell *et al.*, 2012; Hayhurst *et al.*, 2015).

Some of the commonly encountered methodological limitations of diversion literature include the following.

- Weak designs: the lack of an appropriate control group or a valid counterfactual.
- Timing of the study: within the early phases of the programme.

- The data used: reliance on client interview data raises concerns, with low numbers of participants and high levels of attrition, as does reliance on official crime statistics, which can only include recorded or reported crime.
- Limited follow up: unable to examine the effects of the programme in the medium to long term.
- Selection bias: including only those who successfully completed the programme, and not those who failed and were potentially returned to traditional criminal justice procedures.
- Difficulty in comparing results across programmes: due to high levels of heterogeneity and a focus on single programme evaluations.
- The outcomes measured: many studies focus on recidivism and neglect important social outcomes such as employment, housing, relationships and police legitimacy.
- Limited cost-effectiveness analysis (Wundersitz, 2007; Shanahan *et al.*, 2017a).

There is consensus that all operational diversion programmes require ongoing monitoring and evaluation. Evaluations must be designed into newly implemented programmes from the outset to be most effective (Weatherburn, 2018). Future evaluations of these programmes ought to employ more rigorous and robust methodologies that includes appropriate control groups, key mechanisms linked to programme outcomes, long-term follow-up periods and ongoing cost–benefit analysis. Furthermore, there is a need for evaluations 'to take a more holistic approach designed to assess the overall, or composite, effectiveness of the range of drug diversion programs now operating within each jurisdiction' (Wundersitz, 2007, p. 112). The key to an effective system of diversionary schemes is to have in place a wide range of programmes to target different types of client with varying needs across the criminal justice spectrum:

> Evaluations are needed that compare and contrast these /.../ types of initiatives, to determine whether they complement or compete with each other for clients and resources, whether the continuum

of responses is actually working in practice, whether any drug or drug-dependent offenders are slipping through the cracks and whether, in combination, [they] are achieving mutually reinforcing outcomes.   (Wundersitz, 2007, p. 112)

Evaluations of programmes need to also encompass a wide range of social outcome measures, as well as levels of drug use and crime. Furthermore, it is imperative that evaluations establish not just whether an intervention or programme is successful but *how* it works and *under what conditions* and *for whom* is it successful (Pawson and Tilley, 1997; Pawson, 2006). It is essential that programmes establish clear programme logic, that is, 'the mechanisms through which the program is expected to achieve its intended objectives' (Weatherburn, 2018, p. 9), as well as any potential unintended consequences. Decision-makers need to know whether and how a policy or programme can be put in place and what the realistic objectives are.

Net-widening

A concern identified within diversion is the potential for net-widening. Net-widening occurs when mechanisms of diversion supplement the system with new populations or 'widen the net', by increasing the number of offenders in contact with the CJS. This new population of individuals whose behaviour may have previously resulted in an informal action may now be subject to a more formalised response; where failure to comply with programme conditions could result in being returned back into the CJS (Hughes and Ritter, 2008).

Net-widening is of particular concern for young offenders. Diversion of young people from the CJS is based on the recognition that many young people will cease offending of their own accord, with minimal or no intervention. The potential for programmes to formalise and increase contact with these young people, who would previously have been dealt with informally, is also considered as net-widening (Clancey and Howard, 2006).

Previous research has highlighted the potential for some drug court practices to have a net-widening effect, with researchers asserting that 'drug court programs actively encouraged participation from drug users with minor or infrequent substance use' (Lilley, 2017, pp. 678–679). A recent study of drug courts in the US found that drug arrests increased in areas where drug courts had been implemented, suggesting that law enforcement officers increased their attention toward minor drug offences (Lilley, 2017). This finding was consistent with other studies that had found that the proliferation of drug courts, particularly in the US, had not necessarily been associated with reductions in prison populations. While drug courts may reduce the incidence of incarceration as a discrete sanction at trial, when analyses included the time participants spent incarcerated prior to trial, or as part of non-compliance with the programme (as many drug courts use imprisonment as a sanction for non-compliance), there was no evidence to suggest participants spent less time in prison than those processed via traditional means (Sevigny *et al.*, 2013).

Furthermore, Sevigny *et al.* go on to suggest that even if drug courts reduce individual-level exposure to incarceration, the evidence does not indicate that they reduce the overall burden on correctional resources. Those that succeed in drug courts may then avoid prison time and reduce the risk of incarceration on entering the court, but this benefit is outweighed by the fact that those who 'fail' may consequently be sentenced to lengthy prison time that is equal to, or sometimes exceeds, the sentences of those who would not go through the drug court (Sevigny *et al.*, 2013).

There are several conceptual perspectives on why net-widening may occur. The first is a conflict between the objectives of law enforcement and harm reduction, where the increase in drug diversion initiatives is perceived by law enforcement as an attempt to focus resources on drug-related crime as opposed to reduce harm. Second, the increasing popularity of therapeutic jurisprudence, which encourages agents of the CJS to play a more active role in the rehabilitation of offenders, might similarly justify a more 'hands-on' approach from law enforcement or judicial officials (Prichard, 2010; Lilley, 2017). Net-widening could be caused by misrepresentations or misunderstandings of the conceptual underpinnings of drug diversion programmes by law enforcement officers. This makes clear the importance of clearly communicated programme philosophy. While harm reduction, therapeutic jurisprudence and the 'social care model' are all relevant theoretical underpinnings to diversion measures, they must be understood as intended and not misinterpreted.

CONCLUSION AND IMPLICATIONS FOR POLICY

Diversion programmes within the CJS for people who use drugs represent an important part of drug strategies in many different countries. The emergence of diversion programmes signifies a shift away from traditional justice procedures and a recognition of the complex relationship between drugs and crime. Taking a broader social approach, as opposed to a strictly criminal justice approach, addresses the underlying causes of drug use and criminality and has a much stronger opportunity to reduce the harms associated with drug use and crime at both an individual and community level. As argued by Seddon,

> [p]olicy needs to address the broader category of delinquency of which 'drug-related crime' is just one part. In doing so, it needs to position delinquency within wider social processes and engage properly with the deeper aetiological questions /.../ with the aim of regenerating local economies, reducing youth unemployment, providing and maintaining decent housing, improving education services and developing adequate community and leisure facilities.
> (Seddon, 2000, pp. 104–105)

Successful diversion programmes have been shown to have a positive effect on individuals and communities through reducing individual drug use and offending behaviour, as well as improving broader social outcomes. However, to achieve these outcomes diversion programmes must be framed by best-practice guidelines based on empirical evidence drawn from robust programme evaluations. Jurisdictions ought to employ a range of diversion responses for individuals with varying levels of risk and needs, and they ought to include both police-led and court-led interventions. Police-led interventions should target the lower end of the spectrum, in terms of less severe drug use and offending behaviour, and these interventions should more closely resemble true diversion: diverting offenders away from the CJS. Court-based interventions ought to be reserved for offenders with more severe drug use and offending behaviour, where a higher level of supervision and intensity of response is warranted, and draw more upon the therapeutic jurisprudence model of diversion (Wundersitz, 2007).

Integral to a system of diversionary responses is that all those involved in the CJS must have a shared understanding of, and responsibility for, how the system operates. It is highly important that law enforcement do not use arrests to divert minor offenders towards more serious responses, such as drug courts, as this could lead to net-widening and offenders receiving a more intrusive response than if they had been through traditional procedures. It can also replace or displace those offenders with more serious drug involvement and higher needs. The proliferation of, and reliance on, drug courts in the US may cast the net too wide, with evidence indicating that law enforcement activities encourage offenders with minor drug use into drug courts, suggesting that the full range of diversionary options is not being utilised in this context (Lilley, 2017).

From a policy perspective, policymakers and evaluators must always remember that 'the operationalisation of effective diversion is more complex than the functional transfer of knowledge into practice' (Bull, 2003, p. 118). Best-practice guidelines are difficult to operationalise and are only supported to varying degrees by empirical evidence. It is very important, particularly during programme implementation and infancy, that realistic expectations and clear targets are outlined and communicated for what diversion interventions can deliver and achieve (McSweeney *et al.*, 2008). Diversion programmes may be more likely to reduce the harms associated with drug use or the further harm caused by criminal justice intervention, rather than reduce or eliminate drug use altogether. Diversion programmes provide individuals with the opportunity to improve a variety of social outcomes, such as improved health, employment opportunities or relationships, which in turn can have a positive influence on future offending or drug use.

There is a need for clear objectives for diversion programmes based on high-level outcomes (i.e. social outcomes) rather than lower-level process-related objectives (i.e. fewer drug arrests), with particular attention given to the 'feasibility of actually achieving them within the context of what the program has to offer' (Wundersitz, 2007, p. 112). Clear objectives and eligibility criteria alongside consistent monitoring and evaluation are required of programmes to ensure they are meeting realistic expectations and desired outcomes. Diversion schemes have a tendency to take hold and become an entrenched element of the system. The fact that a programme has been established and is functional in one jurisdiction is often used as the basis for an extension of the programme or as the justification for a new initiative (Clancey and Howard, 2006). This demonstrates the importance of in-built evaluation from programme infancy.

Diversion programmes differ internationally, and different countries have unique systems of diversion interventions. Lessons ought to be drawn from different contexts to make the best use of available evidence while also taking into account the local context: 'the globalisation of social policy might well provide beneficial insights but it might also result in homogenous policy transfer with littler consideration of local conditions and populations' (Clancey and Howard, 2006, p. 382). When regarding evidence of best practice there is also the potential for policymakers to focus on 'what works' at the expense of considering unintended consequences and personal harms that might arise – particularly for those who are unsuccessful within programmes due to non-compliance. Consideration must equally be given not just to the potential success of a policy or diversion programme, but also to the practicalities and challenges of putting it into practice (Bull, 2005). Within the field of diversion, setting realistic and achievable targets that are consistently measured and monitored is paramount, to ensure that improved social outcomes for both individuals and communities are achieved.

REFERENCES

Alcohol and Drugs Council of Australia (1996). Best practice in the diversion of alcohol and other drug offenders. In *Proceedings of the ADCA Diversion Forum*.

Andrews, D., Zinger, I., Hoge, R. D., Bonta, J., Gendreau, P., and Cullen, F. T. (1990). Does correctional treatment work? A clinically relevant and psychologically informed meta-analysis. *Criminology* 28(3), 369–404.

Baker, J., and Goh, D. (2004). The cannabis cautioning scheme three years on: an implementation and outcome evaluation. Available at http://www.lawlink.nsw.gov.au/bocsar.

Bennett, T. (2009). The casual connection between drug misuse and crime. *British Journal of Criminology* 49(2), 513–532.

Birgden, A. (2002). Therapeutic jurisprudence and 'good lives': a rehabilitative framework for corrections. *Australian Psychologist* 37(2), 180–186.

Bull, M. (2003). *Just Treatment: A Review of International Programs for the Diversion of Drug Related Offenders from the Criminal Justice System*. School of Justice Studies, QUT, Brisbane.

Bull, M. (2005). A comparative review of best practice guidelines for the diversion of drug related offenders. *International Journal of Drug Policy* 16(4), 223–234 (doi: 10.1016/j.drugpo.2005.05.007).

Clancey, G., and Howard, J. (2006). Diversion and criminal justice drug treatment: mechanism of emancipation or social control? *Drug and Alcohol Review* 25(4), 377–385 (doi: 10.1080/09595230600741388).

Cooper, C. S., Chisman, A. McG., and Lomba Maurandi, A. (eds) (2013). *Drug Treatment Courts: An International Response for Drug Dependent Offenders*. OAS–American University, Washington, DC.

Csete, J., and Tomasini-Joshi, D. (2015). Drug courts: equivocal evidence on a popular intervention. New York. Available at https://www.opensocietyfoundations.org/reports/drug-courts-equivocal-evidence-popular-intervention.

Freiberg, A., Payne, J. L., Gelb, K. R., Morgan, A., and Makkai, T. (2016). Drug and specialist courts review: final report. *SSRN Electronic Journal* (doi: 10.2139/ssrn.2991602).

Hayhurst, K. P., *et al.* (2015). The effectiveness and cost-effectiveness of diversion and aftercare programmes for offenders using class a drugs: a systematic review and economic evaluation. *Health Technology Assessment* 19(6), 1–198 (doi: 10.3310/hta19060).

Hucklesby, A., and Wincup, E. (2010). *Drug Interventions in Criminal Justice*. Open University Press/McGraw-Hill Education, Berkshire, UK.

Hughes, C. E. (2007). Evidence-based policy or policy-based evidence? The role of evidence in the development and implementation of the illicit drug diversion initiative. *Drug and Alcohol Review* 26(4), 363–368 (doi: 10.1080/09595230701373859).

Hughes, C., and Ritter, A. (2008). *A Summary of Diversion Programs for Drug and Drug-Related Offenders in Australia*. DPMP Monograph Series, No. 16. National Drug and Alcohol Research Centre, Sydney. Available at https://ndarc.med.unsw.edu.au/sites/default/files/ndarc/resources/16 A summary of diversion programs.pdf.

Hughes, C., Shanahan, M., Ritter, A., McDonald, D., and Gray-Weale, F. (2014). *Evaluation of Australian Capital Territory Drug Diversion Programs*. DPMP Monograph Series, No. 25. National Drug and Alcohol Research Centre, Sydney. Available at https://ndarc.med.unsw.edu.au/sites/default/files/ndarc/resources/Evaluation of the Australian Capital Territory Drug Diversion Programs.pdf

Hunter, G., McSweeney, T., and Turnbull, P. J. (2005). The introduction of drug arrest referral schemes in London: a partnership between drug services and the police. *International Journal of Drug Policy* 16(5), 343–352 (doi: 10.1016/j.drugpo.2005.06.008).

Lilley, D. R. (2017). Did drug courts lead to increased arrest and punishment of minor drug offenses? *Justice Quarterly* 34(4), 674–698 (doi: 10.1080/07418825.2016.1219760).

Longshore, D., Turner, S., Wenzel, S., Morral, A., Harrell, A., McBride, D., Deschenes, E., and Iguchi, M. (2001). Drug courts: a conceptual framework. *Journal of Drug Issues* 31(1), 7–26 (doi: 10.1016/j.profnurs.2005.11.002).

Lutze, F. E., and van Wormer, J. (2014). The reality of practicing the ten key components in adult drug court. *Journal of Offender Rehabilitation* 53(5), 351–383 (doi: 10.1080/10509674.2014.922155).

McSweeney, T., Hough, M., and Turnbull, P. (2007). Drugs and crime: exploring the links. In *Drugs in Britain: Supply, Consumption and Control* (edited by Simpson, M., and Shildrick, T.). Palgrave Macmillan, Basingstoke.

McSweeney, T., Turnbull, P. J., and Hough, M. (2008). The treatment and supervision of drug-dependent offenders: a review of the literature prepared for the UK Drug Policy Commission. *Policy* March, 88.

Mitchell, O., Wilson, D. B., Eggers, A., and MacKenzie, D. L. (2012). Assessing the effectiveness of drug courts on recidivism: a meta-analytic review of traditional and non-traditional drug courts. *Journal of Criminal Justice* 40(1), 60–71 (doi: 10.1016/j.jcrimjus.2011.11.009).

Nolan, J. L. (2009). Commonwealth contrasts. In *Legal Accents, Legal Borrowing: The International Problem-Solving Court Movement* (edited by Nolan, J. L.), pp. 76–108. Princeton University Press, Princeton, NJ.

Nolan, J. L. (2010). Freedom, social control, and the problem-solving court movement. In *Social Control: Informal, Legal and Medical* (edited by Chriss, J. J.), pp. 65–89. Emerald Group Publishing.

Pawson, D. R., and Tilley, P. N. (1997). *Realistic Evaluation*. Sage, London.

Pawson, R. (2006). *Evidence-Based Policy: A Realist Perspective*. Sage, London.

Prichard, J. (2010). Net widening and the diversion of young people from court: a longitudinal analysis with implications for restorative justice. *Australian and New Zealand Journal of Criminology* 43(1), 112–129. Available at http://journals.sagepub.com/doi/pdf/10.1375/acri.43.1.112.

Reich, W. A., Picard-Fritsche, S., and Rempel, M. (2018). A person-centered approach to risk and need classification in drug court. *Justice Quarterly* 35(2), 356–379 (doi: 10.1080/07418825.2017.1317012).

Russell, P., and Davidson, P. (2002). *Arrest Referral: A Guide to Principles and Practice*. Effective Interventions Unit, Scottish Executive, Edinburgh.

Schwalbe, C. S., Gearing, R. E., Mackenzie, M. J., Brewer, K. B., and Ibrahim, R. (2012). A meta-analysis of experimental studies of diversion programs for juvenile offenders. *Clinical Psychology Review* 32, 26–33 (doi: 10.1016/j.cpr.2011.10.002).

Seddon, T. (2000). Explaining the drug–crime link : theoretical , policy and research issues. *Journal of Social Policy* 29(1), 95–107.

Sevigny, E. L., Fuleihan, B. K., and Ferdik, F. V. (2013). Do drug courts reduce the use of incarceration? A meta-analysis. *Journal of Criminal Justice* 41(6), 416–425 (doi: 10.1016/j.jcrimjus.2013.06.005).

Shanahan, M., Hughes, C., and McSweeney, T. (2017a). Police diversion for cannabis offences: assessing outcomes and cost-effectiveness. *Trends & Issues in Crime and Criminal Justice*, 532.

Shanahan, M., Hughes, C. E., McSweeney, T., and Griffin, B. A. (2017b). Alternate policing strategies: cost-effectiveness of cautioning for cannabis offences. *International Journal of Drug Policy* 41, 140–147 (doi: 10.1016/j.drugpo.2016.12.012).

Social Science Research Council (2018). *Drug Courts in the Americas*. Social Science Research Council, New York. Available at https://www.ssrc.org/publications/view/drug-courts-in-the-americas/.

Tiger, R. (2013). *Judging Addicts: Drug Courts and Coercion in the Justice System*. NYU Press (Alternative Criminology).

United Nations Office on Drugs and Crime [UNODC] (2014). *World Drug Report 2014*. Vienna. Available at https://www.unodc.org/documents/wdr2014/World_Drug_Report_2014_web.pdf.

US Department of Justice (1997). *Defining Drug Courts: The Key Components*. Washington, DC.

Weatherburn, D. (2018). *Outcome Evaluation in Crime and Justice: Notes for Policy Analysts and Program Managers*. NSW Bureau of Crime Statistics and Research, Sydney.

Wexler, D. (2000). Therapeutic jurisprudence: an overview. *Thomas M. Cooley Law Review*, 17.

Wundersitz, J. (2007). *Criminal Justice Responses to Drug and Drug-Related Offending: Are They Working?* Australian Institute of Criminology, Canberra.